SWORD OF THE SPIRIT
A BEGINNER'S GUIDE TO ST. PAUL

Also by the authors:

From Mark Hart

Blessed are the Bored in Spirit: A Young Catholic's Search for Meaning

Ask the Bible Geek: Answers to Questions From Catholic Teens

Ask the Bible Geek 2: More Answers to Questions From Catholic Teens

100 Things Every Catholic Teen Should Know (co-author)

Saintbook (co-author)

From Christopher Cuddy

I Choose God: Stories from Young Catholics (co-editor)

To order, visit our online store at www.lifeteen.com or call 1-800-809-3902

SWORD OF THE SPIRIT
A BEGINNER'S GUIDE TO ST. PAUL

CHRISTOPHER CUDDY
&
MARK HART

The information contained herein is published and produced by Life Teen, Inc. The resources and practices are in full accordance with the Roman Catholic Church. The Life Teen® name and associated logos are trademarks registered with the United States Patent and Trademark Office. Use of the Life Teen® trademarks without prior permission is forbidden. Permission may be requested by contacting Life Teen, Inc. at 480-820-7001.

Cover photography and design by Carlos Weaver

Cover image: sword provided by The Renaissance Store

Special thanks for Esther Trinh, Alissa Roberts and Lisa Epperson for their assistance during the editing process.

ISBN: 978-0-9802362-2-4

Published by Life Teen, Inc.
2222 S. Dobson Rd.
Suite 601
Mesa, AZ 85202
www.lifeteen.com

Printed in the United States of America.
Printed on acid-free paper.

For more information about Life Teen or to order additional copies, go online to www.lifeteen.com or call us at 1-800-809-3902.

DEDICATION

To His Holiness Pope Benedict XVI,

A true shepherd who, like St. Paul, became our spiritual "father in Christ Jesus through the gospel" (1 Corinthians 4:15).

Thank you for your declaration of the year of St. Paul. May the faithful continue to grow in love for this great Saint and for Mother Church through the gift of Her Sacred Scriptures.

And may we all strive, in our own vocations and ministries, for the same humility, boldness and brilliance you display - offering the promise of truth amidst a culture of relativism.

TABLE OF CONTENTS

FOREWORD

It's impossible to imagine what the last two thousand years would have been if St. Paul had not lived at the far end of them. All the years since then have borne the mark of Christianity — the sign of the cross — and so much of what we understand about Christianity, and especially about the cross, we have learned from the great Apostle to the Gentiles.

St. Paul was among the first Christians to set pen to paper to proclaim the Gospel. He looked upon the news of the day, as it unfolded, and interpreted it all in light of God's previous marvels. He took the great heritage of Israel and renewed its language for the New Covenant. St. Paul gave the Church the vocabulary it would, ever after, use to understand the life, death, and resurrection of Jesus.

We have St. Paul to thank for so much of what we call Christianity today. It's not that he was the "founder" of Christianity, as some people claim. But he did play a huge and unique role in the proclamation of the Gospel.

His name from birth was Saul, and he had been a Pharisee — an intensely devout and intelligent man, whose entire life was motivated by the expectation of Israel's Messiah. As a Pharisee, he worked to hasten the day of the Messiah's coming. He went so far as to enforce the strictest fidelity to the Law of Moses, believing that this would bring about the Day of the Lord. It was for this reason that he persecuted the Christians. He thought they were abandoning the God of their ancestors in order to worship Jesus.

As he traveled on his way, Saul met Jesus. (You'll read about that later in the book.) His encounter with Jesus was dramatic, but it wasn't a conversion, because it wasn't a "turnaround," which is the literal meaning of "conversion." It was more of an advance forward on the way. He recognized, then and there, that Israel's expectations had already been fulfilled, the work had been accomplished, the day had indeed been hastened, the messiah had come. It was Jesus.

There was no need for Saul to abandon the religion of the Old Covenant or radically redirect his zeal. Rather, he saw the signs and proclaimed the Day of the Lord, no longer in anticipation, but now in fulfillment.

Of course, this came at no small cost. It was a career-killer for him as a Pharisee. And then he had to endure afflictions and hardships beyond counting — calamities, beatings, floggings, stoning, imprisonment, shipwreck, hunger.

Soldiering on, he traveled the known world to announce a Church that was not just a reservation for the righteous, but was indeed universal, intended for Israel and the nations together.

At some point he began to use the name Paul. Still, his change was not a "conversion." It was not a turning around but a bold charge forward, a rush, a drive. In fact, of all the apostles, it was Paul who most consistently kept the Church from receding back to the safety of a provincial reservation. It was Paul who kept the universal, Catholic vision. It was Paul who proclaimed the power of the sacraments of the New Covenant. It was Paul who confronted the first pope, St. Peter, and urged him to live up to his own infallible papal teaching. In the end, it was Paul who was impelled by grace, together with Peter, to consecrate the city of Rome with his own blood, shed in martyrdom.

Even today, after so many centuries, Paul's letters convey a personality that is overwhelming, a drive that is urgent. It's as if he cannot get the words out fast enough. We sense an excitement, but we can also be frustrated by his maddening compression of language. He rarely takes the time to spell things out, and he assumes that we already know a lot, about the Bible and about the times that he and Jesus lived in. So we shouldn't feel too badly when we find St. Paul difficult. Even St. Peter confessed that, when he read St. Paul's letters, "There are some things in them hard to understand (2 Peter 3:15)."

St. Paul's energy, his richness, and his complexity can challenge us, and we shouldn't be surprised. We are talking, after all, about growth in "the grace and knowledge of our Lord and Savior Jesus Christ" (to steal a bit more of St. Peter's description of Paul's doctrine). Growth means development and change, and that's rarely easy for us. Sometimes it even causes us growing pains.

When we read St. Paul, we can sometimes feel as if we're being propelled forward by a hurricane, a tidal wave, or some other force of nature. But I've got news for you: it's even stronger than that, because it's a force of grace. Look at those maps of Paul's missionary journeys. Ponder those wide swaths that run the length and breadth of an empire. Imagine the momentum that made such progress possible.

And then remind yourself that the same momentum has not diminished. God's arm has not been shortened. When you read St. Paul, when you hear his words proclaimed in the liturgy, you're exposing yourself to the same force: "the grace and knowledge of our Lord and Savior Jesus Christ." And that can only be life-changing.

It can be fearsome, too, and daunting; and for that reason we can be thankful for books like this one, and guides like its authors, whom I count as friends.

Now brace yourself.

Scott Hahn, Ph.D.
Founder and President
St. Paul Center for Biblical Theology

INTRODUCTION

ST PAUL: THE SPIRIT'S SWORD

A Picture is Worth More Than a Thousand Words

Growing up Catholic, I looked at the Bible a lot. Note the verb in that previous sentence — I *looked* at the Bible a lot. It was the *picture Bible* we had in my house growing up, and the *pictures* got a lot of looks…the words? Not so much.

It sat on the third shelf of the bookcase in our family room. Rarely did it come down off that shelf for prayer as, again, we were Catholic and (unfortunately) weren't in the habit of reading the Bible with any regularity. It did come off the shelf for entertainment, however, because the pictures thoroughly intrigued me.

There was one picture in particular that always held my attention, even at only seven or eight years old, called *The Martyrdom of St. Paul*. A quick examination of our family Bible would have shown this to be the picture that got the most "looks." The spine was so bent in that particular place that, when one opened the hard cover, the book almost naturally flipped open right to this picture.

In it, St. Paul is kneeling as his Roman executioner is wielding a sword in the air, just moments before Paul was to lose his head. He was being martyred as the final witness to a life spent serving God. The picture also depicted the presence of an angel, unseen by the Roman soldier but offering visible confirmation of God's presence during a moment of evil's suspected triumph.

The picture was incredible: the colors were vibrant, the figures passionate. And the truth of it was impossible to ignore. Truth takes hold of your soul and your subconscious in ways you may not realize in the moment, but reflect on for years to come. Little did I know that, to this day, when I hear the word "martyrdom," this picture is instinctively the first image that rushes to my mind.

1

At the time, I had no concept of who St. Paul was or what he did. I certainly had no idea why he was being beheaded. I was just a normal little kid and swords (and later, light sabers) caught my attention, and the picture was engaging to my innocent eyes; it drew me in. Years later, I discovered the power of the words contained on the pages surrounding the pictures. Hopefully you have, too.

Martyrdom was the end of Paul's story…his *earthly* story, at least. But the martyrdom of St. Paul might not mean much to you if you haven't really followed the beginning and middle of his story. By "following" Paul's story, I don't mean "read" or "heard" it. I mean *experienced, walked, discerned* and *prayed* it.

Take a moment, now, and ask the Holy Spirit to open your eyes and ears to something new from reading this book. Ask St. Paul to pray with you and for you, that you might gain new insights into Jesus Christ by focusing time and energy into the Scriptures and the life and writings of this great Saint.

Now, let's take a look at how this seemingly random man ended up martyred — how this obscure tentmaker from Tarsus could change the world in such a dramatic way that every corner of it would hear his words thousands of years later, and entire years (see the Appendix) would be dedicated to him. Let's head back to the beginning of his story.

A reading from the Acts of the Apostles:

> "…Saul (was) still breathing threats and murder against the disciples of the Lord…as he journeyed and approached Damascus, and suddenly a light from heaven flashed about him. And he fell to the ground and heard a voice saying to him, 'Saul, Saul, why do you persecute me?' And he said, 'Who are you, Lord?' And he said, 'I am Jesus, whom you are persecuting; but rise and enter the city, and you will be told what you are to do.'
>
> The men who were traveling with him stood speechless, hearing the voice but seeing no one. Saul arose from the ground; and when his eyes were opened, he could see nothing; to they led him by the hand and brought him to Damascus. And for three days he was without sight, and neither ate nor drank (Acts 9:1-9)."

Little Did He Know

How cold and hard the earth must have felt as his body was thrust down upon it. The ground, itself, may have been the only thing colder or harder than Saul's heart that day. How brilliant the light must have been to him and how blinding the vision; that temporary blindness would later offer him *true vision* for the rest of his earthly days.

The roadway was little more than a path of dirt covered with small jagged rocks and pebbles. It was far from a desirable place to lay your head, much less land on it. How humbling it must have been for Saul, powerful Saul, to so quickly go from being the hunter, to the *hunted*. How ironic that he landed upon the earth as he was humbled by God, for both "ground" and "humility" share the same root word in Latin (a language Saul certainly knew).

The dirt caked upon his face. His vision blurred, but his hearing must have sharpened. Saul's companions stood speechless, but Christ did not.

In a flash, everything he knew, everything he had learned during his years of Rabbinical study, were rendered almost irrelevant. In one instant, he went from being certain of his righteousness and superiority among his God's children to staring God in the face and going blind. The revelation was not only one of God's identity or Saul's shortsightedness, but Saul's *self-righteousness* was revealed.

"Why are you persecuting me?" asked his "new" Lord, *the* Lord, Jesus Christ.

How painful those words must have been to Saul. How many the bloodstained memories that must have rushed back to Saul's subconscious. No doubt in his blindness he recalled the faces of those he had hunted down and persecuted, faces like Stephen's. How gruesome the images, how deep the pain, how humbling the guilt overflowing in your soul when you realize you've helped kill your own brothers and sisters, sons and daughters of our God and Father.

Those he had helped condemn, those he had called "apostates" (people who renounce their religious beliefs), he would now call brothers.

Can you relate to Saul, at all? Ask yourself the following questions.

- Do you look at your sins as not only hurting other people (your brothers and sisters), but see your actions as hurting Jesus, himself?

- Is your experience or vision of God as intimate or personal as Saul's?

- Do you feel like God calls you by name, and even *knows* your name?

- Have you begun believing that God doesn't notice you or seem to care about what you do?

- Is your vision of God one of an absent Father who is far from active in your life?

If some of these questions strike a nerve with you (like they do with me) than perhaps your vision of God, like Saul's, needs to change.

The God Saul encountered that day was "different" than the God he had come to know on his own. When Saul was humbled, he was startled; when he was blinded, he began to truly see. That's what grace does — it gives us the eyes of faith.

Saul was about to undergo the greatest change in his life. After encountering Christ face to face in such a profound way, everything about Saul would change…starting with his name.

When the Irresistible Force Encounters a Moveable Object
Many of us like to think more highly of ourselves than we ought. Atheism is a perfect example of man, wounded and self-consumed, thinking more highly of himself than he should. Atheists easily point to "facts" that demonstrate how God cannot be, and put far too much emphasis on their own human logic and intelligence (or lack thereof). In cases such as these, it's pride, not logic, that is the problem. There will always be a certain degree of faith necessary but a hardened heart and a stubborn soul are too consumed with pride to embrace anything with the arms of faith.

Of course, I have yet to meet an atheist who can create a star, flower or giraffe… to say nothing of creating true human life (not cloned) or performing a miracle. The point is that our intelligence, though laughably non-existent compared to God's wisdom (Isaiah 55) can sometimes give us a higher opinion of ourselves than we should have. The Scriptures are filled with verses that warn of such pride and egotism (Romans 12:3, Luke 14:11, Proverbs 16:18, 1 Corinthians 4:6).

Saul was a prideful man. Saul is like me and Saul might be like you, too.

Even though we might picture ourselves as strong and immoveable, the truth is that when we encounter the Irresistible Force (the love) of God, something has to give…something has to change. God gives His love so freely that we are the ones who change; love changes everything. Confronted with the love, mercy and power of God, we are reduced to rubble.

Saul sat blind and quite humbled. Everything he knew up until that trip to Damascus had now changed, but it wasn't just Saul's world that was changing. God was doing something greater, something internal, something far less obvious and far more profound: God was changing Saul's *essence*, the very fiber and makeup of the man. God was re-creating Saul, to a certain extent;

4

He was making Saul new, and Saul signified that by taking a new name. Saul became known as Paul.

Now named Paul, the future saint's understanding of his own vocation and purpose took on new meaning. He was already a man of strong principles and courage, bold and passionate in defending the principles he saw as truth. His zeal had been directed toward a prideful approach and violent end.

Scripture speaks of Saul dragging the early Christians out of their homes and condemning them to death (Acts 8:3). While we shouldn't condone his behavior, it's hard not to admire his passion, especially when so many people are so apathetic about their faith. As one modern philosopher explains, Paul may have been "…moving in the wrong direction, but at least he's moving. It's easier to move a car to the right if it's already moving…than if it's not moving at all."[1] Saul's desired destination didn't change, his route did. His "conversion" was not about changing his focus or goal like most conversions are but, rather, about changing the means in which he pursued it.

Paul's calling and ultimate success (for the Kingdom) should give all of us great hope. No matter how sinful we have been, no matter how prideful we could ever be, God can use us and is willing to use us, if we are willing to change. God has a plan for you (Jeremiah 29:11), a plan He crafted before your conception (Psalms 139:14-16), a plan that only you can fulfill (Jeremiah. 1:5-10).

Paul came to believe in this fact. He didn't just believe it, he preached it:

> "For we are his workmanship, created in Christ Jesus for good works, which God prepared beforehand, that we should walk in them (Ephesians 2:10)."

We are created by God. We are re-created into Christ's image with the hope and expectation that we would do good works, works that God prepared for us beforehand (our vocation).

Often, we cannot clearly see or hear God's plans for us because we are so consumed with our own. God, in His love, finds ways to shake us (Hebrews 12:26-29), though, out of our own "best-laid" plans. Of course, the gentleness or force with which He shakes us is normally a result of our stubbornness and sin. Too many of us, out of pride, run the other way; we choose "the hard way." But, as Saul learned, you can't outrun God. Once shaken, we are broken, and can then be remade more perfectly into His image. The formula goes something like this: shake, break, re-make.

Paul didn't go straight from the road to preaching; he spent years in prayer and discernment, growing in humility and preparation. It was later that he fulfilled his vocation as the world's greatest missionary. The question remains, though, what did Paul have that was so appealing for God to use in this way, for this mission? Was he just a guy with a lot of passion and drive? Just a man with a solid work ethic? He was a Rabbi who knew the law, sure, but he was also a tentmaker who was out for blood. What did God see in this religious fanatic? To understand why Paul was the way he was, we have to understand Saul's background.

Need Change? Can Anyone Break a Pharisee?

It's impossible to understand what a radical change in perspective and lifestyle Paul went through if we don't understand a little bit about the life he lived before his encounter with Christ. Saul was a Pharisee and that is vital to understand before we move forward.

If we were to take a survey of all the Catholics coming out of Mass on Sunday or, better yet, all of the Christians coming out of services on Sundays, the *majority* of people probably wouldn't know much about Pharisees. So, if you don't either, rest easy — you're not alone. Pharisees (and Sadducees) are members of different Jewish "sects" from before, during and after the time of Jesus. Basically, a *sect* is a group of people with somewhat different or "separate" religious beliefs.

The word "Pharisee" comes from a Hebrew word that means "separate"; they separated themselves from most of society, or people considered "sinful," in an effort to stay "clean." In the time of Jesus, they were the "popular religious political party" (John 7:48). They came onto the scene about two hundred years before Christ, when the Greeks were forcing the Jews to abandon their religious practices. What began as a good and necessary thing, however, became a more of a bad thing over time.

What's vital to understand about the Pharisees was that they were very, very "legalist" and followed the Law of Moses in extremely exacting ways (Matthew 9:14 and 23:15, Luke 18:12). They separated themselves not only from Gentiles (non-Jews), but from other Jews as well. While their intentions seemed pure and their creed was solid, their religion was more about form and function than surrender or humility; they obeyed the letter of the law but ignored the spirit of it.

They were very self-righteous (Matthew 9, Luke 18). As a result, Jesus laid into them pretty strongly (Matthew 12:9, 16:1-4). They "supplemented" the law with their own traditions, which took the laws an unnecessary step or two further than even God had designed. They knew the law like the back of their hands but not the front of their hearts. That's why there was such a "rub" with Jesus when He came onto the scene — they believed in the coming of the Messiah, but denied that He was Jesus, even though He fulfilled all of the Messianic prophecies that existed in their Scriptures. If their hearts would have been open, they would have recognized it. When Saul encountered the Messiah in Christ Jesus, Paul embraced the truth with unrelenting passion and urgency.

The Pharisees are not unlike many modern followers of God. Many of them are well intentioned, highly intelligent and very disciplined. They wouldn't miss Mass on a Sunday but, at the same time, don't believe that the Eucharist is the true body and blood of Christ. They know rituals like the Mass, but don't seek to know the purpose or sacrifice "behind the sacrifice."

The Pharisees' worship, their religious practices, their speech, their dress and their attitude all reflected a very cold, impersonal relationship with God and their fellow man. They were still waiting for the Messiah, their Savior, but didn't recognize Him in Jesus when he was right in their own midst; he didn't fulfill their "expectations." This is what Saul came from, but *everything* changed for Saul when he encountered Christ and now- Paul's interior change forced radical change in his exterior life. His life was forever re-directed and changed the moment He met Jesus.

Who Do You See in the Mirror, Saul or Paul?
Have you encountered God in a personal way? Do you know and relate to Jesus Christ in an intimate way? Are you more like Saul or Paul? Do you worship, do you go to Mass out of obedience or out of love?

If you haven't had that "encounter moment" in your life yet, that "Aha!" moment when you just *know* that God is real, Christ is present, and that you're a sinner and you need God's mercy, it's time to look again. What are you doing to give the Holy Spirit a shot at your heart? Are you going to Mass or spending time in prayer? Are you going to Reconciliation or reading the Scriptures? Are you falling on your knees and just crying out to God to save you from your sinfulness, your world, your brokenness and yourself? It's never too late to fall into the arms of God. Prayer is not complicated and it should never be scary. It's not about the words. It is about the posture of the heart. Stop and pray right now and ask God to speak to you.

If you *have* had that "encounter moment" in your life, what have you done about it? Was it a "retreat high" where you said, "I'm yours, Jesus" but didn't follow it with any tangible change? After you encountered God, did your environment change? Did your relationships change? Did your attitude, outlook, habits, dress, speech, conduct, focus, future or goals change? If not, this question has to be asked: "Am I letting God's will guide my life, or am I just looking for Jesus to put his rubber stamp on my own will?" If you've encountered Christ but been reluctant to really jump in and change, now's the time. It's like a "fire sale" for the soul...everything (you know) must go, so that God's will is all that's left.

In either case, a true encounter of Christ is like turning on the light in our souls. Sometimes it occurs on a retreat or at a camp. Sometimes it happens at a conference or at a "talk." It often happens during one of the Sacraments, when "the lights just go on." Most of the time, though, it occurs during times of darkness and suffering. It's in those times, when we are most humbled and most in need, that the light of Christ (John 8:12) beckons us out of our darkness and, like a lighthouse in a storm, guides us safely to shore.

God's constant love requires a response on our part. If we are sincere, that response will be visible in our lives, speech, love, conduct, dress, language, etc. St. Paul reminded his understudy, St. Timothy, of this fact (1 Timothy 4:12). A Christian should be known by their love and their actions, not just by words or titles.

Regardless of where we are right now, our goal should always be to see how we are like Saul — misguided, self-focused, judgmental — and strive to be more like Paul — humble, God-focused, merciful. This doesn't come easily and doesn't happen quickly. It doesn't take a literal "knock you off your donkey" encounter with Jesus to begin your own process of spiritual transformation (change) as Saul had, either. Christ is capable of giving us encounters just as profound as Saul's in moments of silent, prayerful meditation, selfless service or true Christian fellowship.

Your own ongoing conversion and the deepening of your faith shouldn't be judged by the "how" of your encounter moments, as in, "how" God chooses to speak to you, but in the "what," as in "What is Christ calling me to change this day, to leave behind this day, to sacrifice this day?"

And the answer to that question requires being present to the God who is eternally present to us.

A New Portrait of Jesus Christ

You're going to find that St. Paul's writings are very unique. If you've never really studied Paul's epistles (letters) in the Bible before, you might think that they are a lot like the Gospels, recounting stories of Jesus and what He said. Actually, they are quite different.

In St. Paul's writings, you're not going to read about what Jesus said or how He went around doing good works, healing the blind and the lepers, etc. It would have been easy for Paul to talk about these things. Given the time during which he lived and wrote, and how Jesus' works were being carried on orally. There is every indication that Paul, too, knew the stories of the Gospels that had yet to be recorded in their full form.

Why didn't St. Paul record the actions and words of Jesus like his apostolic counterparts, Matthew, Mark, Luke and John? Was it because he was not an eyewitness of the events? No, because Luke wasn't, either. Was it because he wasn't one of the "original twelve" apostles? Again, the answer is not that simple. St. Paul was probably seeing St. Luke everyday while St. Luke was writing his gospel, so it's not as though the events of Jesus' past wouldn't have been on Paul's mind or heart.

What you won't see when you read St. Paul's works, is a historian's focus. St. Paul didn't focus on what Jesus *said* and *did* as much as he focused on what Jesus' words and actions *meant* to everyday life.

Paul focused on Christ's *presence* in his present. Following his encounter with Jesus, he viewed Christ as ever-present, not a historical figure. Paul understood something that many people back then and still today seem to forget: **Jesus Christ is alive** and Jesus Christ is always present. Consider his words to those in Corinth:

> "And he (Christ) died for all, **that those who live might live** no longer for themselves but for him…from now on, therefore, we regard no one from a human point of view; even though we once regarded Christ from a human point of view, we regard him thus no longer. Therefore, if any one is in Christ, he is a new creation; the old has passed away, behold, the new has come (2 Corinthians 5:15-17)."

St. Paul's understanding of Christ *present* dismantles the notion that, following the Ascension, Christ "went back to being God." Many people then and now think of Jesus as a sort of "human costume" that God "wore" for about thirty years. The idea is that God sort of "parachuted" out of Heaven into the manger, worked miracles, was crucified, rose and then flew back up into Heaven and took off the costume.

Nothing could be farther from the truth. Jesus Christ is still Jesus Christ, in Heaven, only in His glorified form. Jesus Christ is "the same yesterday, today and forever" as we are told by the writer of Hebrews (see Hebrews 13:8).

St. Paul didn't want converts to the faith to view Jesus Christ merely as a piece of history. If you are living your faith strictly as a "memorial" to a dead person or a God who is no longer active, where is the motivation for a true relationship, one that is going to grow over time? St. Paul knew and proclaimed that not only is our Lord Jesus alive in Heaven, but that He is alive in His mystical body of believers, the Church, and in His Word and Sacrament(s). After Christ made the truth of His presence in others *so clear* (Acts 9:4-5), Paul could never look at his fellow man the same way. To him, *everyone* was Christ.

In St. Paul's writings, you won't get the résumé of Christ's accomplishments, but you'll find a deeper understanding of the "personality" (for lack of a better term) of Jesus. We say "lack of a better term" because "philosophically speaking, our Lord had no human personality, it's the one human thing he hadn't got."[2] But make no mistake: Jesus is the human face of God. *God is Jesus*. When you see Jesus, you see the Father (John 10:30 and 14:9).

What St. Paul does (and does beautifully) is give us the person of Christ behind the works; he brings to light what it was about Jesus that was so endearing and so moving. St. Paul gives you a glimpse at why so many loved and followed Jesus, the kind of heart and life that made fishermen leave their nets, prostitutes stop sinning and tax collectors repay those they cheated.

When you read St. Paul, you get a portrait not just of how to be "like" Christ, but how to shed your own sinfulness and really become *one with Christ*, or a "little Christ," as C.S. Lewis put it.

The Reason for this Book – What We're Gonna Do

The subtitle for this book is "A Beginner's Guide to St. Paul". Now, it is admittedly impossible to tell you everything you need to know about St. Paul in one book — others have tried.

That is not our goal. When Pope Benedict XVI declared the year of St. Paul rather than the *day* of St. Paul, the Church intuitively taught us something great: growing in spiritual depth and appreciation will take time.

What you're going to read on the pages that follow is the "broad stroke" outline of St. Paul's theology. We're going to take St. Paul's greatest and most sophisticated written work, his *Letter to the Romans*, and use it as a blueprint. The reason for using *Romans* is twofold:

1. *Romans* was one of the last works that St. Paul wrote and, in it, we can clearly see the culmination of years of prayer, preaching and teaching coming together. The result is one of the greatest written works of the Bible and the greatest (non-Gospel) treatise on Christianity the world has ever known. It sums up the thoughts, goals and "thrusts" of all of St. Paul's earlier letters to the groups in places like Corinth, Galatia and Colossae. Put simply, if you "get" Romans, you're going to understand 1 Corinthians, Galatians, Colossians, etc. a whole more.

2. *Romans* is the book that has driven the greatest "wedge" between Catholics and non-Catholic Christians in the past four hundred years or so. Actually, it's not the book itself that has caused the wedge, it is the differing *interpretations* of the truths expressed in the book that has created the rift. If all believers

can understand a few key words, terminologies and concepts, Christians of different denominations will quickly see that our beliefs, though different on certain doctrinal and practical issues, are more similar than different regarding faith and salvation.

Basically, in the pages that follow, we hope to provide you with a portrait of St. Paul's life that is a little different than most books that have come before. We're going to keep things as simple as possible (which is difficult to do with Divinely inspired Scriptures) and speak in more general terms. We're not going to go into exhaustive meanings or deep exegesis — that's not the purpose of this book. Our goal is to give you enough of a basic understanding of St. Paul's core teachings (and enough tools to unpack those teachings) that all of his writings will come more to life for you.

The better you understand the man behind the letters, the one whose pen the Holy Spirit took captive, the better you'll understand not only half the New Testament (which he wrote), but also the Gospels, Mass, and Sacraments, and your faith, vocation and role in God's plan of salvation.

This book is a gift to you, not because we wrote it but because God somehow got it into your hands. God, the Living Word (John 1:1), wants to speak to you through His Word in a new way now. You'll soon see why the Scriptures are "sharper than any two-edged sword" (Hebrews 4:10), because they'll pierce your heart en route to your soul. You'll find, too, why St. Paul calls the word of God the "sword of the Spirit" (Ephesians 6:17). Our hope is that you will also see how St. Paul himself is a sword in the hands of the Holy Spirit, a sword that helps bring life, not death.

He whose earthly life is pierced and killed by the Sword of the Spirit, will live forever.

CHAPTER ONE

THE ONE BEYOND QUESTION: WHO IS GOD?

One of the oldest prayers known to man is a simple meal-time grace. It is immortalized because of its simplicity and remembered because it kind of flows and rhymes: *God is great, God is good, and we thank Him for this food.*

Although short enough for a child to remember and recite, there is a lot of substance to that prayer. It expresses three extremely important points about God: 1) God *is* — He exists. He's not a figment of our imagination; He's real. 2) God is *great*. He is all-powerful and has ultimate authority over everything that He has created. 3) God is *good*. He is a just, righteous and loving God. All of this may seem pretty simple and straightforward, but we probably could spend the rest of our lives studying, praying, and meditating upon God's existence, greatness and goodness (and some guys have!). Don't let it fool you: this is deep stuff.

Life is interesting. Most of us learn about the Lord at an early age. It is usually our parents, grandparents, or friends who first tell us about this powerful being called "God." Sometimes, He's used as a threat: "If you do bad things, God will be angry and He'll punish you." Other times, He's used as an incentive: "God will reward you if you're good." And, still, other times, He is something thrown about as a common curse word.

But this raises the question, *Who*, exactly, is God? Or, even, *What* is God? Is He a cosmic force somewhere up in the sky? An invisible man watching our every move, recording every good (and bad) thing we do? Is He a "celestial Santa Claus" or a "heavenly genie" that has an unending supply of gifts and wishes to grant?

Is He powerful enough to do whatever He wants? Is He considerate enough to help us with the things *we* want? Does He care about us? Is He personal? Is He kind? These are all very important questions that all people ask at least once in their lives. And we're going to look to St. Paul's letter to the Romans for the answers to these and other significant issues.

(Are You) For Real?

If you were to walk down a street in your hometown and perform a random poll, asking "Do you believe that God exists?", most people would say that they do. Atheists — people who deny the existence of God — aren't very common. Sometimes people just have a very small view of God. Other times, they believe that He's somewhere out in space and totally disconnected from our life and world. Very rarely will anyone ever actively deny that there is a "supreme being" somewhere doing something.

You may not like God. You may not care about Him. You may (wrongly) think that He doesn't care about you. But we're going to suggest that it is reasonable to believe that He exists. Again, whether you think He's a power, a spirit, an entity or a force; there are compelling reasons to believe that He is, and this book is written with that assumption in mind.

Why is this? Isn't it remarkable that so many people believe that God exists? How do we know that He's real? Most of us have not heard Him "speak" audibly. We can't see Him looking down at us from heaven. We've never passed Him on the street. There are no divine billboards saying things like "God is real!" And yet somehow we all have a sense that God exists. How can this be?

Good questions! Indeed, how it is that we know that God exists? We don't believe in the tooth fairy. No one has ever seen the Easter Bunny. Most of us eventually discovered that "Santa's elves" were really our parents. But not so with God. People of all ages — old and young — believe in the existence of God. People from all countries and nationalities worship Him. Yet none of us has ever laid eyes upon Him, touched Him, smelled Him, heard His voice. How and why do we know that He's real?

The apostle Paul faced similar questions almost two thousand years ago, and his answers are still relevant to us today. St. Paul taught that even though we don't hear an audible voice from heaven or pass Him on the sidewalk, everyone knows that God is real because He has clearly revealed Himself to us. "For what can be known about God is plain," St. Paul says; and the reason for this is simple: "because God has shown it" to us all (Romans 1:19). The existence of God is not a secret. The question of His reality is not an unsolved mystery. God's presence is not something we have to decode — He made it easy for us. *God has revealed himself to us. He has shown us that he exists.*

But this raises another question: "Okay, Paul, you say that we know God exists because He has revealed Himself; that's all nice and stuff, but how has He revealed Himself? Again, I don't hear a voice from up in heaven shouting 'Hey, I'm up here!' We don't receive heavenly e-mails or text-messages from a divine cell phone. He hasn't faxed us a picture of himself. So *how* has He revealed himself?"

Being the divinely inspired genius that he was, St. Paul anticipated this question and gave a powerful answer. "Ever since the creation of the world his invisible nature, namely, his eternal power and deity has been clearly perceived in the things that are made (Romans 1:20)." How has God revealed Himself to us? *He has revealed himself to us in and through the things that He has made.* We see traces of God in the created world around us.

Who Dunnit?

Detective stories are very popular. It is fascinating for us to learn how investigators gather clues and evidence in order to figure out "who dunnit" — who committed the crime. One of the most common and useful tools law enforcement officials use to catch culprits is the *fingerprint*. If cops discover someone's fingerprints on the murder weapon, chances are pretty good that the person was, at least partially, involved with the crime. The fingerprints show that the person had contact with the scene of the crime. One of the things television shows like *CSI* and *Law and Order* tell us is this: *we always leave behind traces of our presence everywhere we go.* No matter how careful someone is, there will always be a fingerprint, a hair strand, a clothing fiber or something left behind that reveals something about the person who was there.

The same is true with God and the world. When God created the universe, He left behind "fingerprints" of sorts. There are traces of His presence in the world. This was nothing new or revolutionary. The Bible has said this all along. The Book of Wisdom tells us that all created things reveal the existence of their "craftsman" (Wisdom 13:1). Furthermore, St. Paul taught that God designed all things in such a way that people would know that He exists and would seek after Him (Acts 17:26). *The Catechism of the Catholic Church* states this as well: "God speaks to man through the visible creation. The material cosmos is so presented to man's intelligence that he can read the traces of its Creator. Light and darkness, wind and fire, water and earth, the tree and its fruits speak of God and symbolize both his greatness and his nearness (CCC, 1147)."

This is not a revolutionary concept. Is really just plain old common sense. If I hear a knock on the door, I know that someone or something has to be the knocker. If I receive a phone call, there has to be a caller. Whenever something happens, it happens because something caused it to do so.

Things don't just happen by themselves.

The very fact that there is such a thing as *creation* (the universe in which we live) points to the fact that there must be a *Creator*. Something cannot come from nothing. And the fact that there is something at all — and, in our case, many different things in this vast world — tells us that there has to be something that made it (for more on this see CCC, 31-34).

Do We Really (and Always) Get it?

Our knowledge of God's existence is not a "possible" or "hypothetical" knowledge. St. Paul emphasizes the fact that God's existence is "plain" because "God has shown" His existence to all of us (Romans 1:20). The *Catechism* tells us that we can be *certain* about the existence of God by observing His work in creation (CCC, 31). God has shown Himself to us, and His nature has been "clearly perceived in the things that have been made (Romans 1:20)." Everyone gets it. In fact, everyone sees His existence so clearly that they are "without excuse (Romans 2:1)." No one will ever be able to stand before the judgment seat of God and say, "I didn't know You were real because You didn't give me enough clues."

But this raises another question: "Alright, Paul: you say that God exists and that His existence is clearly seen in the created world. It makes sense to me, but there's a slight problem with what you're saying. If God's existence is so obvious and clear, why do some people still seem to miss it?"

Good question. There does seem to be a problem with all of this. God exists. The Bible says we know this because He has clearly revealed Himself to us. But the fact remains: some people still don't believe that God exists. And while atheists aren't very common, a few authors have recently written very popular books arguing that people are foolish if they believe in the existence of God. This is troubling. If God has really so clearly revealed Himself, how is it that people don't always see it?

If there really is a God, then why are there atheists?

St. Paul has some very strong words to say about this issue. He doesn't beat around the bush. The apostle tells it like it is. He says that there have been people who "knew God [but] did not honor him as God," and as a result "they became futile in their thinking and their senseless minds were darkened." This is tragic because although they were "claiming to be wise," they "became fools" in their denial of His existence. St. Paul shoots straight with us and gives us an answer that is razor-sharp in accuracy and precision — so sharp that it's hard for us to accept at times. "For although they knew God they did not honor Him as God or give thanks to Him, but they became futile in their thinking and their senseless minds were darkened. Claiming to be wise, they became fools, and exchanged the glory of the immortal God for images resembling birds or animals or reptiles (Romans 1:21-23)."

The apostle couldn't be any clearer: people *do* know that there is a God. His reality and existence is "clearly perceived" (Romans 1:20), but sin has caused us to become "futile" in our thinking and the light of truth in our minds has been "darkened" to such a degree that we have lost all sense of that which is obvious (Romans 1:21). The truth is so clear, but sin clouds the mind and blinds us to that which is evident.

The answer that St. Paul gives is this: atheism isn't so much a problem of the mind as it is a problem of the *heart*. There are atheists not because God hasn't clearly revealed Himself. There are atheists because of sin and its effects. Atheism is a spiritual problem, not an intellectual problem. St. Paul taught that the only way for you *not* to recognize God's existence is if you don't *want* to recognize his existence. God has clearly revealed Himself — His existence is obvious to any honest person. If someone denies the existence of God, the problem is found in the person, not in God.

How can this be? Why would anyone be so antagonistic to the concept of God? The answer is simple: we "exchange" higher things for lower things. We would rather follow and worship anything but the one, true God who created everything. Although most of us wouldn't worship something as ridiculous as a bird or reptile; our idolatry is just as awful and is ten times more sophisticated. We may not worship our pet parakeet, but we'll let ourselves get sucked into the clutches of pop culture.

Our idols are no longer plants and animals. No, today we worship things like the Internet, movies, sports, food and entertainment. These are the idols that presently enslave our culture. And what makes matters worse is the fact that *many of us don't even realize that we're worshipping false gods*. We're so "in love" with the latest electronic gizmos, sports teams and media gossip that we don't even stop to notice (much less adore) the Creator of the universe. A recent study done by the Bureau of Labor Statistics states that the average American spends less than three minutes a day on "religious and spiritual activities."[3] "Spiritual activities," like prayer, were ranked the most infrequent of all activities. We are so consumed with the things of the creation world that we forget that there even is a Creator! This is the essence of idolatry. We gladly follow anything other than a God who makes demands on us and tell us what to do with our money, our bodies, our time...our lives.

We will examine the nature of sin and its deadly effects more in the next chapter, but suffice it to say that St. Paul warns us to avoid this pitiful insanity. Someone is insane when he or she doesn't see things as they really are. If I were to run down the street screaming, "The unicorns are trying to eat me!", I would be considered crazy. Why? For a very simple reason: unicorns do not exist. There is no such thing as a flying horse with a horn coming out of its head. They are not a part of reality. I would be a fool if I spend my whole life in a fantasy world that doesn't really exist, thinking that the imaginary is real and the real is imaginary.

St. Paul eagerly desired that we not let our view of reality become so distorted that we think that the truth is a lie and that a lie is the truth. Those "claiming to be wise" really become "fools" who exchange "the glory of the immortal God for images resembling mortal man or birds or animals or reptiles" — or movies, sex, Internet or anything else (Romans 1:22-23). The apostle wants to save us from spiritual insanity.

A wasted life is a life lived without worshiping God. A life well-lived is a life spent in His presence and offered for his glory (1 Corinthians 10:31).

God is Great

So far we've seen that God is — that He is real, that He exists, that He's not just a figment of our imaginations. And now we come to another equally important question: *What* or *who* is God? It's one thing to recognize *that* He exists. It's quite another thing to discover what He's *like*. What kind of personality does He have? Is He personable? Does He care about what's going on down here?

Back to the mealtime grace we all learned as kids — "God is great, God is good, and we thank Him for this food" — the next thing we encountered as small children learning this simple prayer is the *greatness* of God. God is great. He is powerful.

The greatness and power of God is essential to our Faith. At each and every Sunday Mass we recite the following words: "We believe in one God, the Father, the almighty, maker of heaven and earth…" It is fascinating that of all the things the Creed could say about God it focuses on His power: "God, the Father, the *almighty*." God is no wimp. He is "omnipotent." That means that He is "all-powerful." The *Catechism* states that "Of all the divine attributes, only God's omnipotence is named in the Creed: to confess this power has great bearing on our lives. We believe that His might is universal, for God who created everything also rules everything and can do everything (CCC, 268)." God's might and power have no external limits. There is nothing greater, stronger or bigger than God.

He is almighty overall, and over *all*.

The Sovereign Author

In order to help us understand just how great God really is, the Church teaches that God is *sovereign*. Unfortunately, "sovereignty" is not a word that is commonly understood in our American culture. This is a shame because it is one of the most profound and comforting things about God. Sovereignty, in its most basic meaning, refers to *authority*. And when we speak of the sovereignty of God, we are referring to His *ultimate and supreme authority over everything*.

Now, authority is something that we are all too familiar with, and many of us shy away from it. The very word "authority" conjures up images of parents, teachers, and police who all inflict their stifling rules and regulations upon us. Most of us would prefer to be left alone so that we can do our own thing. The less authority people exercise over us, the better.

The sovereign authority of God is different from the authority of people, however. His authority is never unjust or oppressive. In fact, the sovereignty of God is one of the most comforting and powerful expressions of His *love*.

The word "authority" is fitting for God. For even in the word itself we can see the word *author*. God is the author of all things — He created everything that exists — and thus He has ultimate *authority* over all things. He is in control. He is fully aware of all that has happened, that is happening and will happen. He has a plan for your life, for the world, and every other thing. The *Catechism* speaks of God being the "sovereign master of his plan (CCC, 306)." From God's perspective, there are no accidents. There is no such thing as "luck" or "chance."

Albert Einstein is famous for saying "God doesn't play dice." God knows all that will happen. He is never surprised by the events that occur. He is in control of everything. He knows everything. He knows how many hairs are on your head (Luke 12:7). God knew you perfectly even before you even created (Jeremiah 1:5).

There are no limits to God's power, God's greatness, or God's knowledge. St. Paul speaks of the "immeasurable greatness of his power (Ephesians 1:19)." In fact, He is the source of true power (2 Corinthians 4:7). If I want to get stronger I have to go to the gym, lift weights and work out. If I want to increase my strength I must work for it. This is not the case with God. He didn't have to "earn" His power and authority. His power is eternal. It has no beginning or end (Romans 1:20). And St. Paul tells us that our faith is "not [to] rest in the wisdom of men but in the power of God (1 Corinthians 2:5)."

This is a critical point. It is easy for us to become smug in our own power, talents, and abilities. This is dangerous — our power is very limited and we are finite creatures. God is infinite. We were created. He is eternal. In fact, God is so great that St. Paul notes that "the foolishness of God is wiser than men, and the weakness of God is stronger than man (1 Corinthians 1:25)." In plain English, the apostle is saying that God could kick anyone's butt even while blindfolded with both "hands" tied behind his back (even Chuck Norris').

God is the creator, the author of everything. He has ultimate authority over all things. His greatness is infinite.

Is God Good?

But this raises another important issue. Someone can be powerful, but that doesn't necessarily mean that he or she is good. Power isn't always a good thing. We've all witnessed people who misuse or abuse their power and authority. Some of the most powerful men in history—guys like Hitler and Stalin—have also been some of the most wicked people the world has ever encountered.

God may be all-powerful, but the real question is this: is God all good?

If you were to ask St. Paul to identify the central theme of his letter to the Romans, he would probably answer "the righteousness of God" (Romans 1:17). Now, most of us have heard the word "righteousness" before, but many of us don't know exactly what it means…especially in relation to God. Well, quite simply, "righteousness" refers to God's *loving faithfulness* to His people in all times and in all places. Even in the face of great difficulty — slavery, sinful rebellion, idolatry — God is always faithful to His people (even when they are not faithful to Him). He promises to be with His people at all times, and He always keeps his promises.

This is very important. St. Paul wants us to know that God is not only great, but that God is also *good*. God does not use his power unjustly. God is a righteous God. He never abuses His authority. It is impossible for God to do evil or to be malicious. His power — His greatness — is always righteous and true. God never excises His sovereignty in a way that is bad or wicked. He is never unjust in his actions. God is *good*. In a word, God is *love*.

It is absolutely essential that we never forget this critical truth: *God's power is His love.* He has no power *but* love. And His love is all-powerful. Again, God is love…infinite love.

Unlike us humans, God will never — and can never — exercise His power unjustly or cruelly. And the reason for this is simple: *God is our Father.* The *Catechism* makes sure to point out that "God's power is loving, for He is our Father" (CCC, 268). This is something that St. Paul notes at the very beginning of Romans when he is greeting his readers: "Grace to you and peace from God *our Father* (Romans 1:7)." And, later on in Romans, St. Paul points to how blessed we are in being given the privilege of calling God, "Abba! Father!"

(Romans 8:15; Galatians 4:6). We aren't just God's "slaves" or "servants," and He is not merely our "owner" or "master." We are nothing less than divinely adopted sons and daughters! We are cherished children of a Heavenly Father.

The *Catechism* wants to make sure that we don't miss this point. It says, very clearly, that "God is the *Father* Almighty, whose fatherhood and power shed light on one another (CCC, 270)." God's power and His fatherly love are not separate things. God's power is His love, and the fire of His love is the mightiest of all powers.

God is an almighty Father from all eternity, but it is important that we remember that He is different from our own, natural fathers. While human dads can sin, make mistakes and let us down; our Heavenly Father cannot — and will never — do any unloving thing to His children. God is the perfect Father. In fact, human fathers should try to imitate God's perfect fatherly example (Ephesians 3:14-15). God is the Father of *infinite* love.

God's authority, sovereignty, and power are all grounded in His perfect *fatherly* love. The Church teaches us that he is a "sovereign God of love (CCC, 2628)" who will never abandon His children. He will never forsake His beloved (Hebrews 13:5). He is always faithful. He can't do otherwise. Everything God does flows out of His infinite, life-giving love.

Life is not a gamble. There is no chance or "randomness" to our existence. While the future may be uncertain to us, we can rest comfortably in the loving control and sovereignty of our Heavenly Father. We can trust His plan, and we can rely upon His fatherly design and plan.

Why Do Bad Things Happen?

Okay, so we've seen that God is all-powerful — that He has sovereign authority of all that is — and we've also seen that God is a righteous and loving Father who does what is good and just. But this leads us to another question: if God is so great and powerful, if He is sovereign and has ultimate authority, if nothing surprises Him, then why do so many *bad* things still happen in the world? Wouldn't a good and powerful God want (and be able) to prevent all of the evils we witness and experience from happening?

This is an important question. Sometimes we get confused when we learn so much about God's power, love, and goodness and then turn on the evening news and see so many things that aren't loving and good. *Where is God in all of this?*

This is something that St. Paul grappled with as well. He was not naïve about the pain and suffering present in the world in which we live. In fact, he was intimately familiar with the trials that accompany life. He experienced many afflictions, endured incredible pains, and suffered tremendous disappointments (2 Corinthians 11:23-33). After experiencing such gruesome beatings and whippings, enduring such tremendous hardships, and suffering great loss and personal pain on numerous occasions, one would be tempted to give up trust in the sovereign love of God.

But such was not the case with the apostle. Far from it, actually. The same St. Paul who suffered more things in a year's time than most of us will suffer in our entire life penned these words: "We know that in everything God works for good with those who love him, who are called according to his purpose (Romans 8:28)."

We will pick up these themes more in chapter four, but for right now we must recognize how St. Paul totally trusted God in all circumstances, and how we are called to trust Him in the same way. Even while undergoing incredible pains, sufferings and afflictions, the apostle did not waiver in his loving confidence in God's power and goodness…and we shouldn't either.

God is great. God is good. And God, in his fatherly love, has a plan for our lives that will work out for our benefit and salvation.

All we have to do is trust and obey.

God, the Father of Mercies…

St. Paul taught that ours is a loving God. He is a father of *mercy* (2 Corinthians 1:3). God is a loving, sovereign Father who knows all things and is working together to draw all men to Himself (John 12:32). Even though we have fallen into sin, God wishes to restore all of us to spiritual life and embrace us in His infinite love (2 Peter 3:9). He is a *merciful* Father who is so great and so good that he is able to save us fallen, sinful human beings from the clutches of death and destruction.

His greatness is seen in his ability to transform our frailty and weakness into His strength and glory. His goodness is experienced in the love he showered upon us by sending His only begotten Son into the world (Titus 3:4).

And his mercy is realized in his willingness to "get His hands dirty" and to continue loving us even when we appear most unlovable. Let us join the Apostle Paul in giving praise to God "who is rich in mercy, out of the great love with which he loved us (Ephesians 2:4)." It is the mercy of God saving us from sin and death that we will begin to examine in the next chapter.

CHAPTER TWO

THE ONE IN NEED OF ANSWERS: WHO IS MAN?

One of the most popular movie series of the last few years has been the Jason Bourne trilogy. These action-packed films tell the story of a secret agent who suffers from amnesia and can't remember anything about his past or his identity. Jason spends all of his time and risks his life in a desperate attempt to answer this question: *Who am I?*

Fortunately, we are not in the same situation as Jason Bourne. Most of us have not suffered an acute case of amnesia and most of us have at least a general idea about our background and family. And although some of us are still in the process of self-discovery as we grow and mature, most of us have a pretty good idea of who we are and where we came from.

Nonetheless, the question we want to raise in this chapter is related to our identity: *Who is man?* What does it mean to be human? What is our *spiritual* ancestry? Where did we come from and where are we going? In short, we want to discover our theological *identity*.

These are some of the most important questions we can ever ask. And there are a lot of different answers given in today's chaotic world. Some people say that we have *no* spiritual ancestry. They argue that we're just a bunch of over-developed organisms with no real eternal significance. Others say that we are *all* gods. This second group argues that *we* — mere humans — are the source of infinite power and being. Amazing as it is, these are things that many people actually believe (perhaps you've encountered some of them yourself)!

It's incredible that some people think we're merely overgrown germs with no real dignity or importance. This mentality is deadly because it leads to a tolerance of heinous practices like stem-cell manipulation, cloning and abortion. It's equally incredible that others believe that we're really God Himself — the be-all and end-all, without any need of a Savior or salvation. It's easy to get confused as we wade through all of the conflicting answers to the question, What is man? And, because of this, let's turn to the Apostle Paul and see how he would answer our question.

St. Paul would say that we are much more special and important than overdeveloped bacteria on the one hand, but that we are far from being almighty God on the other. He would say that we are nothing less than chosen and cherished *children of God* (Ephesians 1:3-6). This is our identity. *We are God's divinely adopted sons and daughters*. This is who we are. This is who we are called to be.

Who Are We (and Where Did We Come From)?

In order to help us understand our source and identity, St. Paul turns our attention to the very beginning — the creation of the world itself. The apostle encourages us to begin our investigation by studying our first parents: Adam and Eve (Romans 5:14).

One of the most famous verses in the entire Bible is Genesis 1:1. "In the beginning God created the heavens and the earth." Many of us have heard the story of creation read during Mass or CCD classes. We've heard about God saying, "Let there be light," (Genesis 1:3), creating the animals (Genesis 1:20-25), and eventually making something — or, rather, *someone* — who was very special to him. In fact, this person was the most unique of all the creatures God had made… and his name was Adam.

Adam and his wife, Eve, were very special. They were God's most prized earthly creatures, and he made them very different from the birds, the fish, and the trees. God made them unique. They were created in God's own *image and likeness* (Genesis 1:26). When we say that something is "like" or "similar" to something else, we mean that they have certain characteristics or traits in common. A daughter is said to be like *her* mother if their hair is the same color, their laugh is similar, or their smile the same angle. My car is *like* your car if we have the same model or brand or year.

"Images" are pictures, snapshots, or representations of something else. If I take a picture of a beautiful sunset on my digital camera, I have just captured an *image* of the sunset. The picture is not the same thing as the actual sunset itself, but it resembles and captures certain aspects of the sunset for us to see and remember even after the sunset has long passed.

This is similar to how Adam and Eve were created in relation to God. They were made in His image and likeness. That means, they resembled God in certain respects and had a certain similarity to Him. Although God is infinitely greater and more powerful than any human person, Adam and Eve still resembled him to a degree.

Adam, though much smaller and weaker and lower, was *like* God in some ways. They had certain similarities. And two of the most important similarities between them are *intellect* and *will*. God created Adam with an intellect to know truth and to understand reality. God didn't want Adam merely to live in the world; he wanted Adam to think, understand, and contemplate the things he saw and encountered. What a gift this was! God gave Adam and Eve intellects to understand truth just like God Himself has an intellect to understand the truth. Granted, God's intellect is infinitely more powerful than Adam's intellect, but his intellect still bore a certain resemblance to God's own intellect.

God didn't stop there, however. He went on to give them another gift as well. In addition to the gift of intellect, God also gave Adam and Eve *wills* with which to *love*. This is also quite remarkable. God didn't want Adam simply to be a walking calculator who could understand reality but yet have no feeling or affections for the things he encountered. He also didn't want Adam to be ruled only by physical desires. God wanted people *both* to know the truth *and* to love the good — each other, and, ultimately, God Himself (who is the Greatest Good).

These gifts of intellect and will were very special. The *Catechism* states that "of all visible creatures only man is 'able to know and love his Creator (CCC, 356).'" Cats and dogs exist, but they can't know and love God. Birds and fish have life, but not a life that can actively worship God. We are so blessed because of all the creatures God created on this vast earth, only man "is called to share, by knowledge and love, in God's own life (CCC, 356)."

And this brings us to our next point…

Created As God's Children
It blows our minds to think back on all of the incredible gifts God showered on Adam and Eve at the very beginning. How good and generous God was to give us intellects to know the truth and wills and to love the good. But as incredible as all of these things are, God wanted to give them something even *more* amazing than even these. God wanted Adam and Eve (and all their descendents) not merely to be His creatures; He wanted them to be His *divine son and daughter*. The greatest gift that God gave Adam and Eve — and the foundation for all of the other gifts they received — was the gift of *divine sonship*. The greatest gift of all was the gift of being His children.

Genesis 5:1-3 makes this point very clear. It states that "when God created man, He made him in the likeness of God" (Genesis 5:1). *No duh. We've heard that a million times*. But wait, it gets interesting: the Bible then says that Adam "became the father of a son in his [Adam's] own likeness, after his image, and named him Seth" (Genesis 5:3). This is vitally important: God made Adam and Eve in his own image and likeness. And, later, Adam had a son (Seth) and his son was born in Adam's image and likeness. There is an unmistakable parallel going on here between God and Adam. As Adam came from God in God's image and likeness, so Seth came from Adam in Adam's image and likeness. Hence, in a very real sense, to be created in the "image and likeness of God" is to be God's son, just as to be born in Adam's "image and likeness" is to be Adam's son.

Adam and Eve were created not as mere creatures but as God's beloved children. *They were God's divine son and daughter.*

What They Had

We've covered a lot of ground so far. God created Adam and Eve to be very special. He made them in His own image and likeness. And we saw that being made in the image and likeness of God has two primary meanings: 1) it means having an *intellect* and a *will* to know the truth and to love the good, and 2) it means that Adam and Eve were God's *divine children*.

These were tremendous gifts from God. They enabled Adam and Eve to live in loving relationship with each other and also with God Himself (CCC, 357). Adam and Eve had a natural perfection. They lacked nothing. They had it all. They lived in a beautiful garden and had a painless life where all of their needs were met. Most importantly, however, they were created "good (Genesis 1:31)" and lived in *"friendship"* with their Creator and in *"harmony"* with themselves and all of the created reality around them (CCC, 374).

They walked with their Heavenly Father in the cool of the garden and experienced His serenity. There was no pain or suffering. There were no marital "spats" between Adam and Eve. Everything was peaceful.

This type of life and existence is difficult for us to envision. Problems, pain, and suffering abound on our every side. Why was it that Adam and Eve had it so good while we have it so bad? Well, the main reason for this difference between our lives and their (initial) lives is something known as the state of *original justice* (CCC, 376). Because Adam was God's divine son, he was filled with *grace* from the very beginning of his life and existence.

But what is grace? We often sing the hymn "Amazing Grace" at Mass, but sometimes we're not sure what this grace really is (and why it's so "amazing"). The *Catechism* teaches us that grace is nothing less than our "participation in the life of God" Himself (CCC, 1997). Grace is God's own being, life, and power imparted to our human souls. It is the great gift of sharing in God's own divine nature (2 Peter 1:4).

This makes sense when we think about our own life and family. We receive life from our parents. We receive their human nature (their "human-ness"). This is what it means to be father: to pass on one's nature to one's offspring. A cat passes on cat life to his kittens. A dog passes on dog life to his puppies. And a human passes on human nature and life to little babies.

In a similar way, when God created Adam and Eve as His divine children, He also shared His own *divine life and nature* with them as well. From the very moment of their creation Adam and Eve were filled with the fullness of God's grace, of His divine life and power (CCC, 375).

The grace of God is powerful stuff! It flowed through their "spiritual bloodstreams" and affected every part of them (body and soul). The grace that they received enabled them to live life free from sin and temptation. There were no sinful passions or urges in Eve. Adam didn't have to struggle with lust or irrational rage. Their intellects were fully in tune with truth and reality, and their wills were fully committed to good and loving behavior. And they had the ability to control their bodies in such a way that they never had to struggle with many of the disordered urges we have to struggle with.

All of this was in fine and proper order because they were God's children — children created in His image and likeness, children filled with His divine life and power. They were "naked, and were not ashamed (Genesis 2:25)." Lust was not a problem. They had no sin in their hearts. They were totally pure. They were also *immortal*. Death was not something they were required to face. Work was easy and enjoyable for Adam and Eve. There was no pain, suffering, or struggle to their lives. And, finally, Adam and Eve — because of their close relationship with their Heavenly Father — had *infused* knowledge. Learning was easy for Adam. Because of the grace and purity he possessed, Adam's intellect was more powerful than we can imagine. God gave them the knowledge they needed (Sirach 17:5). In a very real sense, Adam would have made a genius like Albert Einstein look like a kindergartner.

Remember: the reason Adam and Eve had all of these "superhuman" (or what is known as "preternatural") gifts was because they were God's children. They had His grace — God's own divine life and being — animating and activating their own life and being. God's power flowing through their "spiritual veins" is the reason for the incredible abilities of their intellect, will, and bodies.

God's grace was the "engine" that kept everything working.

What They (and We) Lost

You may be getting a little frustrated as you read this. It almost feels unfair to us, doesn't it? Adam and Eve had it made! Everything they could ever want was practically handed to them. They had it so easy.

Why do we have it so tough? Why can't it be that easy for us, too?

The answer to this question is a small word — only three letters — but it had a devastating effect on Adam and Eve and all who came after them (i.e., you and me). The reason for all of the problems and difficulties we now face is *sin*. Adam and Eve eventually forfeited all of their many gifts because they sinned and disobeyed the Lord.

Fall From Grace

Remember, the most important gift God gave Adam and Eve was divine sonship — the gift of His grace, with His divine life residing within them. This was the foundation for all of the other gifts they had received. Infused knowledge, painless life and peaceful harmony were all dependent on their status as God's children. If they were to lose this grace and reject His life, all of the other gifts would vanish.

God warned them about this early on in their existence. Shortly after He created Adam and Eve, God gave them very clear instructions: "You may eat of every tree of the garden; but of the tree of the knowledge of good and evil you shall not eat, for in the day that you eat of it you shall die (Genesis 2:17)." Death would be the inevitable result of sin and disobedience. But this was not just any kind of death. This death would be the worst kind of death imaginable — spiritual death. The death God warned them about was the loss of His divine life animating their souls. Literally, in Hebrew (the original language of the Old Testament), God says that they would "die die" if they disobeyed. This was not an accident on the part of the writer. God did not have a stuttering problem. The word is repeated twice to emphasize the seriousness of the death that would result. This death wouldn't be small or trivial. It wouldn't even be merely physical. This death would be the worst of all deaths: it would be *spiritual*.

God was telling Adam and Eve that to sin would be to commit spiritual suicide.

Tragically, as we all know, Adam and Eve did not heed the Lord's warning. They would go on to put their trust in themselves rather than in God's word; and they would fall from grace into a state of sin from which we are still recovering (CCC, 398). As soon as they ate from the tree of the knowledge of good and evil, disobeying God, they lost the divine life and grace which had so wonderfully dwelt in their souls, and their harmonious bliss was disrupted (CCC, 399).

It is important to remember that God's love did not change through this tragedy. God is love (1 John 4:8) and he is the same yesterday, today, and forever (Hebrews 13:8). However, like the most malignant cancer, sin destroyed the life Adam and Eve enjoyed and extinguished the power of grace in their souls. God didn't change. Adam and Eve changed — for the worse.

Sinister Realities

What exactly is sin, anyway? Most of us grew up with a list of do's and don'ts imposed on us by our parents and teachers. And this is how many of us still understand sin today. We view it as God's rules and regulations. We are good when we do good and follow the rules. We are sinning when we break His rules and "commandments."

This is true to a point. Sin, in a general sense, is anything — thought, word or action — that offends God or violates the lawful order he has instituted. The Greek word for "sin" used by St. Paul is the word "hamartia," which means "to miss the mark." There is a very real sense in which sin is "missing," or not meeting, the expectations God has set up.

It is important that we emphasize the word *miss*. Although we often think of sin as being a "mark" or a "stain" on the soul, we need to remember that sin is not *something*. Evil has no substance to it. Rather sin is the *absence* of something that should be present. It is the lack of the love and grace that we need to survive. Sin is really *no thing* — it is nothing where there should be something. It is the absence of God's grace and love influencing our lives. We sin when we act in ways that are contrary to God's truth and love.

St. Paul begins his comments on all of this by noting that "sin came into the world through one man (Romans 5:12)." The first sin of Adam and Eve resulted in what is known as the *state of original sin* — the state of spiritual death and the loss of divine sonship. Spiritual death occurred the moment Adam and Eve disobeyed God. The apostle pulls no punches in noting that "death [came] through sin (Romans 5:10)." Death was not what God had in mind. It was not what He wanted for His children. And, like a deadly disease, sin and death "spread to all men (Romans 5:12)."

God wanted life for His children (Genesis 2:7). He wanted them to have joy, happiness, lasting and eternal pleasure. But, through and because of sin, death came into the world. The soul in which God had originally infused His life, love and power was now empty of His divine presence. It was spiritually dead. It was hollow and empty… God's loving presence was gone. Their sin resulted in the "death of the soul (CCC, 403)."

In their disobedience, Adam and Eve committed spiritual suicide. They expelled God's loving presence from their souls. They rejected the gift of divine life — the greatest and most foundational gift God had given them. The *Catechism* states that Adam and Eve immediately lost the "grace of original holiness (CCC, 399)." They rejected the gift of divine sonship. And when this happened — when God's loving presence no longer animated their souls — everything fell apart. All of the other gifts, like infused knowledge, comfort of life and immortality, were gone. Not only were they now spiritually dead, but they would also (eventually) die physically as well. From that point on, "death reigned (Romans 5:14)."

We tend to view sin as just minor, insignificant things. But sin is gripping. Sin is deadly. Sin enslaves. Through their disobedience, we became "slaves of sin (Romans 6:17)" — slaves of death. It was our master. It reigned in our hearts. It mercilessly kept us captive, bound to death, away from the light.

Christ Our Savior

Fortunately, this wasn't the end of the story. The drama of our Christian faith is not a tragedy; it is a story of reconciliation, healing, and eternal joy. There are no surprises to God. He is sovereign. He knew what was going to happen, and He had a plan to set things right…and not just right — He was going to make things infinitely better (Genesis 3:15)!

St. Paul says that our Heavenly Father knew what was coming and "chose us in him [Jesus Christ] before the foundation of the world, that we should be holy and blameless before him (Ephesians 1:4)." Did you catch that? It says that God chose — that He *predestined* (Romans 8:29) — us before the foundation of the world. This is remarkable! That means that God already had a plan for how to make things better even before you or I were blimps on the cosmic radar. God had a plan even before He created Adam and Eve. God is never caught off guard. He knows all. He sees all. And He is working all things together for the good of His children. (Romans 8:28) Nothing can stop His plan of mercy and love.

St. Paul goes on: "He destined us in love to be his sons through Jesus Christ, according to the purpose of his will, to the praise of his glorious grace which he freely bestowed on us in his beloved (Ephesians 1:5-6)." Hold the phone. Stop traffic. The apostle just said something that is absolutely incredible. He just made a comment which is cosmically revolutionary. Re-read that passage again: "He destined us in love to be his sons through Jesus Christ, according to the purpose of his will, to the praise of his glorious grace which he freely bestowed on us in his beloved." Did you catch the incredible statement? Many of us become so accustomed to hearing these types of verses that we almost become numb to them. This is a real shame because St. Paul just said something that should knock you out of your seat (no joke).

The phenomenal statement is this short phrase: "He destined us in love to be his sons *through Jesus Christ* (Ephesians 1:5)." Whoa! This is unbelievable! Okay, okay...some of you are probably scratching your heads in bewilderment right now, asking, "So what's the big deal?" Well, let's take a look...

Justification: (Adopted) Sons in the (Eternal) Son

Adam and Eve had it pretty good in the Garden of Eden, no doubt. All their needs were met. They had superhuman abilities, but, even more so, they had the gift of divine sonship. They were God's children. This gift was priceless. No one can "earn" or "buy" sonship (especially God's), but they had it...it was given to them as a gift.

Nonetheless, as awesome as Adam and Eve's sonship was, it doesn't even begin to compare to the sonship of God's *Eternal Son*. Adam was God's son by grace. The Eternal Son (Jesus) is God's Son because he's "eternally begotten of the Father." *He is God Himself!* Everything that the Father has (and is) is given to the Son. The Son is one in being with the Father. Thus, his divine sonship is infinitely more glorious, splendorous, and incredible than Adam's sonship for this very simple reason: the Eternal Son of God *is* God!

And the incredible thing is that we don't merely "go back" or return to the type of sonship that Adam and Eve had from the beginning. No. As cool as that might sound, St. Paul tells us that we now receive an even greater sonship — we receive *sonship through Jesus himself.* This is mind boggling. Our heavenly Father has so loved us that He has given us an incredible gift that is even more powerful and glorious than the gift He had given Adam and Eve at the very beginning.

God gave us Himself: Jesus. And Jesus himself gives us to his Father.

This teaching is called the doctrine of "justification." The *Catechism* states that through our Baptism we participate in the "grace of Christ (CCC, 1997)" Baptism is the sacrament which unites us to Jesus. In Baptism we become one with him (Romans 6:3-4). And, as sons and daughters of God in the Eternal Son of God we can "call God 'Father,' in union with the only Son (CCC, 1997)."

We have received a grace and blessing even more beautiful than the gift received by Adam and Eve: we are sons and daughters of God *with and in* the Eternal Son of God. One of the greatest councils in the history of the Catholic Church defined justification as a "translation from that state in which man is born a child of the first Adam, to the state of grace and of the adoption of the sons of God through the second Adam, Jesus Christ, our Savior (Council of Trent [session 6, chapter 4]).” When we are justified, we are *declared* and *made* divinely adopted sons and daughters of God (1 John 3:1). This doctrine of “divine sonship” is at the heart of the Catholic understanding of justification.

St. Paul says that Jesus is the new and “second Adam (Colossians 2:9).” Where Adam failed, Jesus succeeded. Where Adam sinned, Jesus obeyed (Luke 22:42). Where Adam died in sin, Christ rose to life in glory (Romans 6:4). And the life that Adam lost in sin, the Eternal Son has given us even more abundantly in love.

Please note that we recognize that our Protestant brothers and sisters have a different understanding of the doctrine of justification. But since we can't go into exhaustive detail here, we've decided to limit our discussion to the Catholic understanding (which we believe is most consistent with the writings of St. Paul).

The Gospel

This is the “Gospel,” the “good news” of our Faith (Romans 1:1-6). The good news that St. Paul spent his life preaching was the good news of Jesus Christ, and the hope we have to be children of God with and in him. “The wages of sin is death, but the free gift of God is eternal life in Christ Jesus our Lord (Romans 6:23).”

Of all the promises and gifts that God could give us, nothing compares with the glory and splendor of being His divinely adopted children *in Jesus*. This is something we could never earn (CCC, 2007) in the same way we can't “work” our way into someone's family. We can't “pay” someone to make us his children — being a son or daughter (even in a human family) is a priceless gift. Nothing we could ever do on our own would obligate God to make us members of His divine family. He does so purely out of His love and mercy (CCC, 2008).

We are sons and daughters who can rely upon our Heavenly Father in all things. We have a merciful Father who is willing to take us by the hand and dust us off when we slip and fall. Our Father never grows tired of hearing our little voices speak to Him in prayer — no matter what time it is — and He will never tune us out — no matter how stupid we think we sound.

Our Father in Heaven is sovereign. Nothing catches Him off guard. No need or request is too great for Him to fulfill. He's got the whole world — and every aspect of our lives — in the palm of His loving hands. He never rejects His children when they call. He never abandons us in our weakness. In fact, it is when we are most weak, and are forced to rely upon Him, that we are most strong (2 Corinthians 12:10).

"God shows his love for us in that while we were yet sinners" — sinners who had rejected the gift of divine sonship — "Christ died for us (Romans 5:8)." What incredible love and amazing grace! How glorious it is that, when we were so lost and distant, Jesus came and died so that we might live with and in him. It is from the Cross that we receive his life-giving love. It is through the Cross that we have faith in his mercy. The Eternal Son of God came to earth, lived, died, and rose again so that we might "obtain the glorious liberty of the children of God (Romans 8:21)." Jesus came to set us free. He came to liberate us from slavery to sin (Romans 6:7) so that we could embrace the loving bond of righteousness (Romans 6:18).

> "For all who are led by the [Holy] Spirit of God are sons of God. For you did not receive the spirit of slavery to fall back into fear, but you have received the spirit of sonship. When we cry, 'Abba, Father!' it is the [Holy] Spirit himself bearing witness with our spirit that we are children of God, and if children, then heirs, heirs of God, and fellow heirs with Christ... (Romans 8:14-17)"

This is the Gospel — the "good news" — that Jesus made possible for and in us. What a gift this is! What a life which is ours to live! And what an "identity" we have received...

> "Amazing grace, how sweet the sound
> That saved a wretch like me!
> I once was lost, but now am found
> Was blind, but now I see."
>
> —John Newton

CHAPTER THREE

WORDS CANNOT EXPRESS: HOW GOD AND MAN RELATE

When God "Touched Down"

There is probably no more famous verse in Sacred Scripture than John 3:16: "For God so loved the world that He gave His only Son, that whoever believes in Him shall not perish but have eternal life." It's on bumper stickers and billboards, on coffee cups and t-shirts and, of course, on poster boards in every end zone of every football game. It's so popular, in part, because most Christians feel that it "sums up" the whole story of salvation.

It is a powerful and straightforward verse, one that St. Paul assuredly would have agreed with and preached often. There is one word in the verse, however, that the devil can sometimes twist to confuse people, even Christians…it's the word "world."

Sometimes it is tempting to think that God doesn't think of us "personally," but only collectively. And while God does absolutely think of us as one body, which we'll discuss more later, it's important — no, make that *essential* — to understand that God thinks of us and loves us personally, too. Yes, God so loved the world, but how different does the verse read when we make it personal? Try it. "For God so loved *me* that He gave His only Son, that I *would believe* in Him, not perish and have eternal life."

For St. Paul, it was personal. It should be for us, too. Although God does relate to us in cosmic ways and worldly events, He is intimately connected to us. Even if God knew that every other living being until the end of time would have rejected His love, He still would have mounted that cross and died, just for you. Paul believed that fact and his preaching showed it.

Sometimes it's difficult for us to grasp this truth about how and why God became man, but the Incarnation (Latin for "made flesh") is vital for us to understand as we move forward. The Incarnation, when God took flesh and "dwelt among us" (John 1:14), is a mystery, but it is a mystery to be meditated upon, not solved. Often times it creates conflict within us because we approach it strictly from our mind and don't let our heart or soul get involved. We need mind and heart and soul, however, if we wish to understand how God relates to man, for God gave us all three and calls us to give all three back to Him (Deuteronomy 6:5, Matthew 22:37).

The Incarnation — It's Not "For the Birds"

I remember the first time that this truth of "God become man" really came to life in my mind, heart and soul, simultaneously. I heard a story that really changed the way I looked at the Incarnation — it's a simple story, often shared around Christmas time. It was made famous by radio celebrity Paul Harvey, when he read:

> "The man to whom I'm going to introduce you was not a scrooge, he was a kind decent, mostly good man. Generous to his family, upright in his dealings with other men. But he just didn't believe all that incarnation stuff which the churches proclaim at Christmas Time. It just didn't make sense and he was too honest to pretend otherwise. He just couldn't swallow the Jesus Story, about God coming to Earth as a man. "I'm truly sorry to distress you," he told his wife, "but I'm not going with you to church this Christmas Eve." He said he'd feel like a hypocrite. That he'd much rather just stay at home, but that he would wait up for them. And so he stayed and they went to the midnight service.
>
> Shortly after the family drove away in the car, snow began to fall. He went to the window to watch the flurries getting heavier and heavier and then went back to his fireside chair and began to read his newspaper. Minutes later he was startled by a thudding sound...Then another, and then another. Sort of a thump or a thud...At first he thought someone must be throwing snowballs against his living room window. But when he went to the front door to investigate he found a flock of birds huddled miserably in the snow. They'd been caught in the storm and, in a desperate search for shelter, had tried to fly through his large landscape window. Well, he couldn't let the poor creatures lie there and freeze, so he remembered the barn where his children stabled their pony. That would provide a warm shelter, if he could direct the birds to it.
>
> Quickly he put on a coat, galoshes, tramped through the deepening snow to the barn. He opened the doors wide and turned on a light, but the birds did not come in. He figured food would entice them in. So he hurried back to the house, fetched bread crumbs, sprinkled them on the snow, making a trail to the yellow-lighted wide open doorway of the stable. But to his dismay,

the birds ignored the bread crumbs, and continued to flap around helplessly in the snow. He tried catching them...He tried shooing them into the barn by walking around them waving his arms...Instead, they scattered in every direction, except into the warm, lighted barn. And then, he realized that they were afraid of him. To them, he reasoned, I am a strange and terrifying creature.

If only I could think of some way to let them know that they can trust me... That I am not trying to hurt them, but to help them. But how? Because any move he made tended to frighten them, confuse them. They just would not follow. They would not be led or shooed because they feared him. "If only I could be a bird," he thought to himself, "and mingle with them and speak their language. Then I could tell them not to be afraid. Then I could show them the way to safe, warm...to the safe warm barn. But I would have to be one of them so they could see, and hear and understand."

At that moment the church bells began to ring. The sound reached his ears above the sounds of the wind. And he stood there listening to the bells – 'Adeste Fidelis' - listening to the bells pealing the glad tidings of Christmas. And he sank to his knees in the snow."

This story has been read and shared countless times over the years, in books and on radio shows, in newspapers and on television programs in almost every imaginable language. Why? Sure, it's a good story, but what makes the story so popular? Is it because we all have loved ones who we wish were more into their faith? Is it because we've all questioned the existence of God before and wondered if He really cares about us, personally? Or is it that we are fascinated by how God, the unmoved Mover and uncreated Creator, makes His presence known to us? The question demands an answer, an answer you probably already know.

In the Flesh

Why did God become man? Why did the Word become flesh (Incarnation)?

You know the answer. In fact, you say the answer weekly. There is a line in the Nicene Creed that we pray at Mass; finish this phrase "...begotten, not made, one in Being with the Father. Through Him, all things were made..."

What's next? That's right, you got it: "...for us men and for our salvation, He came down from Heaven." That's the short answer to the question. That is why God became man. God became man for our salvation. God is love and *true love* works for salvation.

So, *what* are we supposed to learn from Christ (New Testament) that we couldn't or didn't learn about God before Christ's birth (Old Testament)? These were the questions that Paul, an educated and respected Pharisee, had to come to terms with in his own life. St. Paul explained it to the people in Philippi like this:

> "Christ Jesus, who, though he was in the form of God, did not count equality with God a thing to be grasped, but emptied himself, taking the form of a servant, being born in the likeness of men. And being found in human form he humbled himself and became obedient unto death, even death on a cross (Philippians 2:5-8)."

These words contain very deep truths. God took flesh. Basically, He became what we are to give us what He is…He came down to us so that we could get back up to Him. Through the Incarnation, God "meets us where we are at," walking and pointing us to where we need to go. In Christ Jesus, we have a God who is not afraid to get His hands dirty.

The Incarnation is simultaneously a simple truth and a profound mystery, a beautiful and joyful mystery. Our Church "unpacks" this truth even further (CCC 456-463), offering us four distinct reasons that God emptied Himself and took on flesh in Christ Jesus.

First, Jesus came to *reconcile* us with God. Next, Christ came that we might know God's *love*. Thirdly, Jesus came to model holiness. Lastly, Christ came that we would become "partakers in the *divine nature*" (enter into communion and receive divine sonship). We've discussed these ideas a little bit, already, and we'll continue to dive deeper into them, as St. Paul did. Suffice to say, these truths offer a very different perspective of God than most people were used to, St. Paul included. When he came face-to-face with Jesus, everything changed. The God St. Paul thought he knew wasn't who God really was, at all. Paul immediately became aware of his own sinfulness and the need he had for a savior. That is what the Gospel should do for us, too, still today. The Gospel comforts the afflicted, yes, but the Gospel should also afflict us when we're too comfortable. Paul got a wake-up call…the Gospel did for him what it has been doing for centuries since, it offered him the unparalleled gift of self-awareness.

Self-Awareness: The Key to True Holiness

The "good news" of God's forgiveness is often not seen as very good in modern culture. How could this message of justification through Christ not be considered good news, much less *great* news? Well, in a world and a modern culture that doesn't really believe in sin, what good is forgiveness? Why do we need a doctor if we're not sick? Why would I need a "Savior," since "if it feels right" than I must not be a sinner?

The Gospel means "good news" because it contains not only the bad news about sin, but also the good news about salvation. The Gospel (and all of Scripture) is inspired by the Holy Spirit, whom Pope Benedict XVI wisely referred to as "the soul of our soul." It's in this way that our soul is moved by the words (and works) of Sacred Scripture. The same way a baby responds to his or her parents' voice long before they can understand the actual words being spoken, our souls respond, even leap (Luke 1:41) when the Holy Spirit breathes truth into us. Through the reading and, more to the point, *living* of the Gospel, the Holy Spirit invites us to heightened new levels of awareness of self.

This newfound self-awareness necessitates a decision on our parts to the following question: "Am I going to continue to live for myself (Adam) or am I going to surrender my life and live for God (Christ)?" Every decision in life offers you a choice: to be like Adam in Eden and choose yourself, or like Christ in Gethsemane, choosing the Church: two gardens, two choices, drastically different results. This was the choice Paul explains in great detail in chapters five and six of his letter to the Romans.

Again, if we recognize our sin and are humble enough to admit it, the decision is quite easy. The Gospel helps us do both, admit sin and live humbly. If we were writing this out in steps, it would read something like this:

Step One - Encounter the Gospel
Step Two - Realize there is a God
Step Three - Admit that it is not you
Step Four - Acknowledge that Christ is God
Step Five - Admit that you are in sin
Step Six - Realize that you need a Savior
Step Seven - Repent and Reconcile
Step Eight - Believe in the Gospel
Set Nine - Change the way you live
Step Ten - Share the Gospel with others so they can encounter it

Our awareness of not only God's sovereignty and mercy, but our "new" self-awareness of our own incredible pride and sinfulness, leads us to an incredible decision…

To Repent or Not to Repent – That is The Question
Many believe that repentance means "saying you're sorry to God." While that definition is not incorrect, it's not complete. So, let's take a deeper look.

While repentance is a movement of the heart and not a strictly "logical" decision, sometimes it helps to approach it in more logical terms. Imagine repentance as a 180-degree movement. Picture yourself standing in a hallway, gazing down the corridor. You're staring into darkness; behind you is a bright light. Now, as you turn your body ninety degrees, darkness is now on your left and brightness on your right. The ninety- degree turn putting darkness and light into your peripheral vision is the first half of repentance, the turning away from darkness (sin), but you still have a ways to go. It's not enough to stand still between the two, you must keep moving toward the light.

Incidentally, this is where most people get "stuck" during the Sacrament of Reconciliation. It's in this "movement" that the heart and mind can sometimes fall into conflict. If, for instance, you've ever confessed a sin because you feared the consequences but weren't really, heartfully sorry for the sin, you got stuck in the hallway and didn't complete the turn. For the Sacrament to be valid, for the sins to be absolved and for the grace to really take root, we must be truly *contrite*.

What does "contrite" mean? Contrite comes from a Latin word meaning "worn down." Basically, when we've been worn down by our guilt and our sin and we heartfully and humbly admit our wrongdoing with remorse and penitence, we are contrite. The church even offers us guidance, providing us with a prayer to utter called the *Act of Contrition*. Part of that prayer is us begging God for the grace and strength not only to avoid those sins in the future, but to avoid the *environments, relationships* and *occasions* that lead to those sins.

Repentance is the proper (and humble) response to that new self-awareness mentioned earlier. It's only with the help of God's grace and a truly penitent (repentant) and humbled heart that you can make that second ninety-degree turn toward the light of Christ. When we can make that second movement toward the light, we are consumed by God's grace, which allows us to live out our lives in amazing ways.

Virtue-all Reality: Staying Focused on the Light
So, the Incarnation is how the Timeless one entered time and space, in human form, "emptying Himself"(Philippians 2:7) to become like us in all things, "yet without sin (Hebrews 4:15)." *This is how God relates to man,* through Jesus Christ, the "one mediator between God and man (1 Timothy 2:5)." And we understand that it is through Jesus that we are now justified, as we discussed in the last chapter. But what does justification "look like" on a daily basis? How does that change the way God and I relate, much less the daily way I "live?" How do I protect my "state of grace," live a contrite life and allow Christ's light to shine through me?

Put very simply, once justified God now endows us with virtues, to help us become more like Christ. Most specifically, Paul points to the greatest of all virtues, the three theological virtues of faith, hope and love (1 Corinthians 13:13) as the greatest gifts that God endows to those who are justified. So, how does this work?

Through the Incarnation, God blesses us with divine sonship (which we discussed earlier):

> "…God sent forth his Son, born of woman, born under the law, so that we might receive adoption as sons. And because you are sons, God has sent the Spirit of his Son into our hearts, crying, 'Abba! Father!' So through God you are no longer a slave but a son, and if a son, then an heir (Galatians 4:4-7)."

Now, through the grace of divine sonship, we are enabled to live out the virtues. A chapter later in St. Paul's same letter to the Galatians, he lists several of the virtues as fruit of the Holy Spirit:

> "…the fruit of the Spirit is love, joy, peace, patience, kindness, goodness, faithfulness, gentleness, self-control…(Galatians 5:22-23)."

So, what, exactly, is a virtue, and how does it work?

Virtue comes from the Latin word *virtus*, meaning "excellence." Its root is *vir* (Latin for "man"). Virtues are the way in which man reaches his highest excellence or moral perfection. All virtues are founded on the greatest virtue of love. While there are dozens of virtues, there are principally seven that receive the greatest amount of attention in Catholic teachings. We've already mentioned the theological virtues of faith, hope and love. In addition, there are the cardinal virtues of temperance (moderation), prudence, justice and fortitude. Out of these seven are born the other virtues like chastity, humility and patience.

A virtue is a habitual and firm disposition to do the good. In other words, to be all that you are called (and designed) to be by God your Father (Matthew 5:48), you have to tap into and unleash the power of God's grace within you, by virtue of the virtues. Virtues are acquired and strengthened by the repetition of morally good acts, meaning the virtues, like muscles, become stronger with exercise.

The Big Three
St. Gregory of Nyssa said, "The goal of a virtuous life is to become like God." That is exactly the point St. Paul was trying to make (Romans 5:1-11).

> "Therefore, since we are justified by faith, we have peace with God through our Lord, Jesus Christ. Through Him we have obtained access to this grace in which we stand, and we rejoice in our hope of sharing the glory of

God. More than that, we rejoice in our sufferings, knowing that suffering produces endurance, and endurance, produces character, and character produces hope, and hope does not disappoint us, because God's love has been poured into our hearts through the Holy Spirit that has been given to us (Romans 5:1-5)."

Now, if you got lost reading that, don't feel bad. The book of *Romans* is the most poetic, beautifully written and (somewhat) complex of any of the books of the Bible. Each sentence contains a lot of deep stuff, so don't feel bad if get a little lost your first few times reading over it. Let's break this down into a few pieces.

"Therefore, since we are justified by **faith**, we have peace with God through our Lord, Jesus Christ (Romans 5:1)."

Remember how we said that being justified brings with it the "big three" theological virtues of faith, hope and love? Well, this verse is showing us that, by faith, we have access to God and we will live at peace with Him. It's not just saying to have "faith" that He is real, but that our faith in Him should bring us peace, every day, that He loves us and is behind us, cheering us on to Heaven. The grace we need to get there is available to us, at all times.

"Through Him we have obtained access to this grace in which we stand, and we rejoice in our **hope** of sharing the glory of God…and hope does not disappoint (Romans 5:2, 5)."

This verse is reminding us that God keeps His promises, that is what hope is — believing in God's promises for you. God is trustworthy and He promises great things for those who have lived for Him, as Paul shares with the early Church (1 Corinthians 2:9). Pope Benedict XVI shared powerful insight into the theological virtue of hope in his encyclical *Spe Salvi*, ("In hope we are saved").

"More than that, we rejoice in our sufferings, knowing that suffering produces endurance, and endurance, produces character, and character produces hope, and hope does not disappoint us, because God's **love** has been poured into our hearts through the Holy Spirit that has been given to us (Romans 5:3-5)."

These verses tell us that when we live a virtuous life, especially in the face of suffering, that we demonstrate true love, which comes from the Holy Spirit's presence in our hearts. Notice, too, that virtue helps us endure suffering and it builds character.

Did you notice how faith, hope and love are all *active?* Virtues aren't "philosophical" or theoretical; virtues are practical and tangible. What is even cooler is that the virtues within us are purified (and elevated) by divine grace

(CCC 1804-1839), meaning that through God's grace, the virtues can literally transform us from sinners into saints. Again, you might be thinking, "Okay, that *sounds nice* in theory, but how does it work *practically* and what do they have to do with God?"

Grace: The Ultimate Transformer

While we've already discussed justification and our adoption not only *by* God, but into the very *life of God*, you still might be a little "lost" on the word grace. Remember, grace is God's life, God's very life, in us.

Grace is how God makes us more like Him. Grace powers virtue. Grace is how God *transforms* man. That is not to insinuate that we are like "Transformers" who change from one thing to another and then back again. No, the hope of grace is that we change for the better, for good. God doesn't just want to transform our outer appearance, like a robot in a movie. No, God wishes to transform us from the inside out. "Grace is God leaning forward and stooping towards man".[4] Grace is how we truly become "partakers in the divine nature (2 Peter 3:1)." Grace undoes what was done in Eden but it also extends to us who God is in Heaven.

As we've already noted, Adam's sin led us into slavery and Christ's redemption led us out. Paul explains this in detail, showing the parallels and contrast between Adam and Jesus (Romans 5:12-21). Both lives had a huge impact on the world, but the similarities really end there. As he puts it, "…(though) one man's trespass led to condemnation for all men, so one man's act of righteousness leads to acquittal and life for all men (Romans 5:18)." Paul was trying to show that the grace of Christ more than makes up for the sin of Adam. The power of grace is unparalleled and unstoppable. He even goes on to say that "…where sin increased, grace abounded all the more (Romans 5:20)."

What does this mean, you may ask? It means that no matter how much we sin, God's grace is always there in abundance. As Paul reminded the people in Corinth, "(God's) grace is sufficient" and "power is made perfect in weakness (1 Corinthians 12:9)."

So, in effect, what God is saying is, "Don't be overwhelmed by sin. As much sin as you may be immersed in, there is always more grace, I've got you covered." Of course, grace doesn't just "cover" us — it consumes us.

Drowning in Sin or Drowning in Grace?

So, one might believe that's great news, but then later wonder: "If God's grace gets poured out so much when we sin, why not just sin more and release a whole bunch of God's grace?" That idea is rooted in reverse logic and, as error-filled as it is, it's not a new way of thinking. St. Paul dealt with similar thinking and he warned the people in Rome against it.

> "Are we to continue in sin that grace may abound? By no means! How can we who died to sin still live in it? Do you not know that all of us who were baptized into Christ Jesus were baptized into his death? We were buried therefore with him by Baptism into death, so that as Christ was raised from the dead by the glory of God the Father, we too might walk in newness of life (Romans 6:1-4)."

Here, Paul makes it very clear that the very purpose of grace is not only to forgive us of past sins but to assist us in our efforts to avoid future sins (can anyone say, repentance and contrition?). The grace pours out and overflows in absolution, during the Sacrament of Reconciliation, for just this reason. The Sacraments — all the sacraments — were instituted by Christ, Himself, as outward signs that bring *grace*.

In Baptism, we die to sin and are freed from its bondage. What that means is that it no longer has power over us. One of the elements/symbols at Baptism is water. Your body is comprised mainly of water. You can live longer without food than you can without water. Get the idea? We need water to live, but Baptism is about a lot more than water.

Some people have the mistaken idea that the waters of Baptism are just about "washing away" original sin. Yes, they do that, but it's about so much more than that. Baptism doesn't just erase sin; it destroys death and it welcomes you into the family. Through Baptism you are not "cleaned off," you are re-created. In the Sacrament of Baptism we are made new; we are joined to Christ. Our sins are put to death and our souls filled with life. In this way, the physical sign of water embodies the death to old life and the rising in new life. Likewise, every time we bless ourselves with holy water, it should remind us of when we received the reality (not merely the "symbol") of new life in Christ at our Baptism. When we bless ourselves upon entering the Church, we renew our baptismal vows, vowing to die to the philosophies and mistruths of the world and living only for God.

Can you imagine how different our Church and our world would be if we *really embraced* the truth, importance and beauty of Baptism, beyond a "ceremony" or a cute little baby in a white dress? St. Paul wanted everyone to understand the intense and amazing ramifications of what occurs at Baptism, reminding us:

> "So you also must consider yourselves dead to sin and alive to God in Christ Jesus (Romans 6:11)."

Christ's didn't just die "for my past sins." He died (and rose) that you and I might die to sins (present and future) and fully live (present and future), for and with God. As we mentioned earlier in Chapter One, creation naturally reflects and points back to its Creator. Our bodies and, indeed, our very lives, are arrows that point to the source of our life. It is God who created us and God who we are designed to reflect. If God gave us the gift of our bodies and souls, as arrows that (are supposed to) point others back to Him, are we going to use our bodies for His glory or for sin (read Romans 6:12-14 and CCC 2819) ?

Is Your Master a Who or a What?

How about one more story?

"It was the 1800s and a young miner who had recently struck it rich in the gold rush was on his way back East. As he stopped in New Orleans to rest, he noticed a crowd of people gathering for some kind of event. He approached the crowd and quickly learned they were there for a slave auction. He heard a gavel bang on wood and a man exclaim "Sold!" just as a middle-aged black man was taken away.

Next a beautiful young black girl was pushed up onto the platform and made to walk around so everyone could see her. The miner heard vile jokes and comments that spoke of evil intentions from those around him. The bidding began. Within a minute (because of her beauty), the bids surpassed what most slave owners would pay for a black girl. Finally, one man bid a price that was beyond the reach of the other. The girl looked down.

The auctioneer called out, "Going once! Going twice!"

Just before the final call, the miner yelled out a price that was exactly twice the previous bid. An amount that exceeded the worth of any man. The crowd laughed. The miner opened up the bag of gold he had brought for the trip. The auctioneer shook his head in disbelief as he waved the girl over to him. The girl walked down the steps of the platform until she was eye-to-eye with the miner. She spat straight in his face and said through clenched teeth, "I hate you!" The miner, without a word, wiped his face, paid the auctioneer, took the girl by the hand, and walked away from the still-laughing crowd.

Stretching out his hand, he said to the girl, "Here are your manumission papers. The girl looked at the papers, then looked at him, and looked at the papers once again.

"You just bought me...and now, you're setting me free?"

"That's why I bought you. I bought you to set you free."

The beautiful young girl fell to her knees in front of the miner, tears streaming down her face. "You bought me to set me free! You bought me to set me free!" she said over and over. The miner said nothing. Clutching his muddy boots, the girl looked up at the miner and said, "All I want to do is to serve you—because you bought me to set me free!"[5]

It's an imperfect analogy as all analogies regarding God's infinite and perfect love are, but it does demonstrate some sound principles regarding human nature. The point we must take and ask ourselves, however, is the point St. Paul was getting at, namely, "Who is your master and why do you serve him?" He sounds a lot like Christ (Matthew 6:24).

Sincerely ask yourself whether you serve God in your decisions. When you are deciding what to do this weekend, are you seeking to please God or yourself? When you are deciding "how far to go" with the people you date, "how much to drink," "whether or not to look at pornography" or "what to wear," who has the deciding vote — you, or God? Who is the *true* master of your life, God or sin? Paul is asking a difficult question and it deserves an honest response. He is reminding us that God died and rose for us, that we would love and serve Him.

It wouldn't make sense to have a new master purchase you and still work for the old master, would it? We were purchased with the blood of Christ (1 Corinthians 6:20, 7:23). Rising with Christ, spiritual resurrection, means that God is our new master, one who loves us and has freed us. He is the One Whom we ought to serve, out of love. That's what he's talking about when he says,

> "Do you not know that if you yield yourselves to any one as obedient slaves, you are slaves of the one whom you obey, either of sin which leads to death, or of obedience, which leads to righteousness? But thanks be to God that you who were once slaves of sin have become obedient from the heart...and having been set free from sin, have become slaves of righteousness (Romans 6:16-18)."

Sin might sound "fun" at times. Sin might feel "good" at times. But, ultimately, all sin does is kill you. St. Paul was so clear on this point that he offers one of the most clear, yet startling verses recorded in all the Bible saying that, "the wages of sin is death". If the master you serve is sin, the payment for your services will be your death.

So, what is the cure for death? The answer lies in the rest of the verse: "For the wages of sin is death, but the free gift of God is eternal life in Christ Jesus our Lord (Romans 6:23)." Eternal life is the cure for death, and how do we obtain eternal life? Grace. St. Paul, then, understood the transformative power of grace and the need that we all have for it. Grace offers us true freedom and true life... new life.

Don't Just be a "Good Person," be a Christian

One of the greatest modern lies is that Christianity is about being a "nice" person. Countless masses of Christians, Catholics included, think that living as a Christian means "not rocking the boat," being "polite" and "keeping the peace at all costs." The problem with that is it leaves no room for authentic love, because an indispensable part of love is truth. Rather than say what needs to be said, many modern Christians proclaim the "gospel of nice" to not upset close friends at school or family members around the Thanksgiving dinner table. That approach, however, is not consistent with the Gospel (Luke 12:53).

One modern Catholic writer put it this way: "The harsh truth is that Jesus isn't calling you to be a good person. Jesus Christ is calling you to be a *new* person, a new creation (Galatians 2:20), not just converted in mind but transformed in body and spirit. That means admitting that the life you currently lead might not be the life you're called to lead. It means acknowledging that there are areas of your life in which you won't let the Lord be the Lord."[6]

Living as a new Creation means that we "hate and avoid sin now *not out of fear of punishment* (the former motive) and *not simply out of gratitude* (Luther's answer, but not St. Paul's) but (we avoid sin) *because of who we are, Christ's."[7] One could say "I avoid sin because it's just not me." We belong to Christ. We are "little Christs," as St. Augustine would say. Love is what unites us to Him, not obedience or fear, but authentic love. We are connected by the power of His love. In an authentic, selfless love of Jesus, we allow Him to be far more than just our healer, teacher or miracle worker…He is our Savior. Jesus Christ didn't just save us from the punishment for sin, He saved us from sin, itself, so that we would never again have to be mastered by it. Love is what conquers sin.

To recap, *this is how God and man relate*. God wants man to become more like God and get "back to Him." He shares the good news (Gospel) with us about Jesus Christ and His resurrection. The good news, in turn, demands a response from us, the wise (and humble) response is repentance. Once we repent we need to seek out God's grace (beginning with Baptism) and become more aware of the sin that binds us and pushes out God's grace. We must respond to our newfound freedom in Christ by living out our identity as new creations in Christ. As new creations, we ought to work for salvation, as He does, avoiding sin, speaking truth and putting our faith into action. Living as Christ also implies that our faith will be active, that our faith will inspire works born out of love.

Again, you might be saying to yourself (as those Paul preached to probably said), "I really do want to live for Christ, but what happens when I'm not at Church, a conference or camp or on retreat? What happens when I'm 'coming down from the mountain' and I'm not surrounded by my friends who believe the same things I do? What happens when I am at work and I'm the odd one out, with no community of support? What happens when I am forced to face those same relationships, environments and temptations to sin and my 'retreat high' is gone?"

St. Paul knew you'd ask that, too. It's almost as if he'd heard the same problem(s) before. That's why his advice is so practical and so timely, even today, and that's why we move ahead to Chapter Four.

CHAPTER FOUR

LOSING THE FAKE I.D.: HOW MAN RELATES TO HIMSELF

We began our study in Chapter One by examining a well-known meal-time prayer. However, as famous as this prayer may be, there is another prayer which is *even* more famous. And while this particular prayer doesn't rhyme like the meal-time grace, it carries a certain power and depth with which no other prayer can even begin to compete. The reason for this is simple: *it came from the lips of our Savior himself.* Without doubt, the most famous prayer of all time is the "Our Father."

We say the Our Father at each and every Mass. It is beautiful. It is mystical. It is personal. It is deep…and, to be perfectly honest, it can be a little perplexing at times. There are certain parts of the Our Father which just don't seem to "fit" what we would expect in the Christian life.

The prayer starts off good enough — "Our Father, who art in heaven, hallowed be your name" — and it goes on to ask that the Lord's kingdom come, that His will be accomplished, and that our needs be met. So far so good. But the puzzling part comes near the end: "lead us not into temptation, but deliver us from evil." *Whoa!* "Lead us not into temptation"? Where did this come from? Why do we need to *ask* for this? Isn't it a given?

Why am I Still Tempted?

One of the most troubling things new Christians face is the persistent reality of sin in their lives. Some people experience a deep and profound conversion to Christ, return to the Church and the Sacraments with renewed vigor, and commit themselves to a life of holiness and truth. Their hearts are on fire with the love of and for God. Other people might come back from a retreat or conference overflowing with joy, feeling as though Christ's presence is radiating from their pores. They then re-enter the routine of their day-to-day life and eventually, as time goes on, they notice that their spiritual passion begins to diminish. The light slowly fades. The sparkle begins to darken. And they are confronted with the same sins, struggles and temptations they faced before their conversion.

This can be incredibly discouraging. Sometimes people even question whether they had a real or authentic encounter with God at all. Perhaps they just imagined everything. Maybe it wasn't as powerful as they had originally thought. Surely if they *truly* encounter Jesus Christ, sin and temptation will stop being a problem, right?

Well… not exactly. As nice as it would be, sin and temptation remain a constant battle even after a conversion to Christ. Jesus knew that this would be the case, and that is why he instructed us to ask for divine help in avoiding the lure of evils which surround us. "Lead us not into temptation" is not a trivial request; our Lord wants us to make this a petition from the bottom of our hearts. Temptation is real…even for the Christian. One could argue *especially* for the Christian. Like it or not, the battle against sin is a battle we will fight our entire lives.

Sinner-Saints

Sometimes it is frustrating to read through the Bible. We learn about so many people of great faith, and we can grow discouraged when we compare our lives to theirs. Most of us haven't raised anyone from the dead, cast out demons, or miraculously cured the sick. Far from it. Most of us struggle with depression, boredom, lust and lukewarmness. It almost seems unfair. Everyone in the Bible is doing great things with deep faith…and we're doing jack! It just seems to come so easy to them.

Why can't holiness be that easy for all of us?

Well, it may surprise you, but the simple truth of the matter is *it really wasn't all that "easy" for the people in the Bible to follow God, either.* Yes, the Biblical saints had profound encounters with the grace of God, but they also had profound difficulties to work through too. Everyone (but Mary) has to struggle with the real presence of sin and temptation in their lives.

Even St. Paul.

This may be difficult to believe. St. Paul is almost like a "super apostle," always proclaiming the truth, converting people to Christ, and performing miracles. But it's true: St. Paul struggled with sin and temptation just like you and I. And this isn't something we have to figure out or "deduce" on our own. St. Paul admits it himself.

Speaking about all people of all generations, the Apostle describes the tension between good and evil that we all face. Grace is real, it is powerful. It saves — transforming fallen sons of Adam into beloved sons of God (Romans 5:12-15; 1 Corinthians 15:22, 15:45) — but the fight is still real. Sin is still present. Temptation must still be resisted.

Romans 7:15 says something to which we can all relate: "I do not understand my own actions. For I do not do what I want, but I do the very thing I hate." St. Paul understands the struggles we face. There are times when sin seems to overpower us. We want to follow Jesus, we want to abandon ourselves to the power of his love and grace, but the flashy lights of the world are too great for us to resist…and we fall. This can be the most painful experience for the Christian. Here we are, baptized followers of Christ, striving to obey his commandments, desperately seeking the peace of his healing touch, and yet sin remains and we still have to go to Confession…we still have to fight against the "old nature (Ephesians 4:22-24)," the bad habits and the addictions which still plague us.

There are times when we almost feel like "spiritual schizophrenics" — religious Dr. Jekyll and Mr. Hyde's. We know that sin is deadly. We know that Christ is our only hope for lasting joy and happiness. We believe what the Bible says and what the Church teaches, and yet we still stumble and fall. Our bodies, passions, and disordered desires drive us away from holiness and we land painfully in sin.

The battle between good and evil isn't just fought "out there" in the world around us. No, the battle is also fought "in here," *within* us, and it is literally a fight between supernatural life and death.

St. Paul understands this battle we all face. He understands that it's almost like there's "another law at war with the law of my mind and making me captive to the law of sin which dwells in my members (Romans 7:23)." We know the truth and the good with our mind — we sincerely "delight in the law of God" in our inmost being (Romans 7:22) — but our fleshly appetites urge us to do the very things we despise.

It is "immortal combat" in the most literal sense of the phrase. It is a war for our very souls.

Fighting the Inner-Fight

The "inclination towards sin" that we all experience is called *concupiscence*. It is the almost involuntary urge we feel towards sinful thoughts and actions. The *Catechism* says that although "holy Baptism" has "cleansed us" with forgiveness that is "full and complete," we still have to face the "weakness of [human] nature." Our humanity is still susceptible to the lure of temptation and sin. Hence, "we must still combat the movements of concupiscence that never cease leading us to evil (CCC, 978)." Concupiscence, the "inclination to evil (CCC, 405)" which everyone (but Jesus and Mary) has to face, "makes man's life a battle (CCC, 409)." We are at war with the forces of evil. Thus, we must stand firm in Christ, our Savior and resist the pull of sin in our lives.

St. Paul echoes the painful cry many of us feel deep down in our bones as we fight temptations: "Wretched man that I am! Who will deliver me from this body of death? (Romans 7:27)" Again, the answer is Jesus: "Christ Jesus has set me free from the law of sin and death (Romans 8:2)."

Jesus Christ is the only one who can free us from the power of sin. We must run to him.

Our Only Hope

"What can I do about this?" you may ask. "I'm trying to follow Jesus with all of my heart, but I just can't seem to stay away from the pull of sin. You don't understand how hard it is. Pornography, drugs, alcohol, illicit sex, gambling, stealing, gossiping, lying — all of these things just have a grip on me, and I've been trying to fight it but I can't break the power it has over me. I just can't do it…"

There are several things that can be said in response to this very real plea for help. First of all, yes, as hard as it may be to believe *we do understand how hard it is*. Both of us, along with the Apostle Paul, understand the reality of the fight against sin. We struggle the same way you do. It's not easy for anyone to live in this materialistic and pornographic culture of death. Each morning we have to get up and beg the Lord for the grace and strength to fight the world, the flesh and the devil just like you.

Trust us, temptation and sin is very real to us as well. We have fight like anyone else; and, sadly, sometimes we fall. And this brings us to our next point.

You're right: you — we — can't do it. We'll lose every time. But there is hope. This battle can be won! Immediately after St. Paul mourns the pull of sin, he raises his hands to heaven and praises our Heavenly Father for the hope he has given us: "Thanks be to God through Christ Jesus our Lord! (Romans 7:25)." This is the exact reason why Jesus came to earth in the first place; he came to release us from our bondage to sin. "But thanks be to God, that you who were once slaves to sin have become obedient from the heart… having been set free from sin, (and) have become slaves of righteousness (Romans 6:17-18)."

We can't do it ourselves. We will fall every time if we rely exclusively on our own strength and resources. But thanks be to God for a mighty, powerful Savior who can overcome every obstacle and defeat every enemy. St. Paul goes on to say that "there is therefore now no condemnation for those who are in Christ Jesus. For the law of the Spirit of life in Christ Jesus has set me free from the law of sin and death (Romans 8:1-2)." Christ has the power to overcome every addiction, heal every wound, purify every thought and restrain every evil impulse. The answer to our dilemma — our weapon in this fight — is Jesus himself.

Although sin does remain a challenge even after Baptism, it does not have the upper hand. If we entrust ourselves completely to the grace of Christ we can resist the forces of evil.

> "Let not sin therefore reign in your mortal bodies, to make you obey their passions. Do not yield your members to sin as instruments of wickedness, but yield yourselves to God as men who have been brought from death to life, and your members to God as instruments of righteousness. For sin will have no dominion over you, since you are not under the law but under grace (Romans 6:12-14)."

Grace is the key. The life of Christ imparted to us through the sacraments is the answer. Sin will beat us every time if we fight alone; but, if we cling to Christ and rely on his saving grace and power, sin will not be able to destroy us.

The grace of Christ is our greatest weapon in the fight against sin. Grace and sin are like oil and water. They can't co-exist. They are completely incompatible. And the surest way to expel sin is to fill up on grace through the Sacraments. This is the reason why we confess any mortal sins before we receive Jesus in the Eucharist. We want our souls to be filled with the fullness of grace so that we can fully receive the King of Grace, Jesus.

Run to Christ. Receive his grace. And sin shall be defeated.

Meeting Christ in our Times of Need

But this raises another question: "Okay, how do I 'run to Christ' when I'm being tempted? I mean, it's not like he's sitting in my living room or walking down the street outside my house or something... where do I meet him? How can I find him in my times of need?"

Good question. Our Lord isn't in "just one place." Jesus is not restricted to geographical locations. If I am sitting in a coffee shop in Pittsburgh, I can't simultaneously be sitting in an L.A. movie theater. The reason for this is simple: my body is limited to one place at one time. God, on the other hand, has no such limitations. He is in the Pittsburgh coffee shop and in the L.A. movie theater — and in every other single place — at the same time with no problem whatsoever. He's God. He's what is known as *omnipresent* (he's simultaneously at all places). There is no location that escapes his gaze or presence (Jeremiah 23:23-24; Acts 17:28). He knows all, sees all and is in all places.

This should be a source of great comfort for us. Whenever we face temptations and difficulties, all we need to do is call on his name (sometimes out loud) and run to our Savior (in prayer and worship). Jesus knows how challenging this life can be — he lived it! The Bible tells us that "we have not a high priest (Jesus) who is unable to sympathize with our weaknesses, but one who in every respect has been tempted as we are, yet without sinning."

When the Son of God became man, he experienced every challenge that we face (except he didn't sin). And because of this we are compelled "with confidence (to) draw near to the throne of grace, that we may receive mercy and find grace to help in time of need (Hebrews 4:15-16)." This is a remarkable Scripture passage. It doesn't beat around the bush. With great clarity it reminds us that Jesus himself underwent temptations. He knows firsthand what it's like to undergo such trials. He doesn't have to imagine how hard it is; he knows. He experienced them.

However, unlike us, Jesus remained firm in his commitment to truth and love throughout his life (and death). He never once conceded to even the slightest sin. He was sinless from beginning to eternity. This is good news for us. We have a Lord who knows how powerful temptation can be, and yet is even more powerful than the greatest of temptations. Because of this we need to rely on him for help and assistance. We must draw near to him, to his "throne of grace," so that we can receive "help in (our) time of need (Hebrews 4:16)."

The three primary ways we draw close to Christ are through the *Sacraments* (especially the Eucharist and Confession), *prayer* and *reading the Bible*. The point we keep bringing up is simple yet essential: *we can't do it on our own; we need Jesus to help us resist temptation and free us from the power of sin.* St. Paul is adamant about the fact that only Christ can give us the "glorious liberty of the children of God (Romans 8:21)." We need Jesus at every second of every day. Whenever we feel *even the slightest urge* to look at pornography, go to the party or accept the bottle, we need to *flee* the scene, *get down* on our knees, and *call out* to our Savior; asking him to give us the strength and power that only he can give.

And when we fall — as all of us do from time to time — we need to run to the healing power of Christ found in the sacrament of Confession. After discussing the presence of temptation and concupiscence in the Christian life (CCC, 978), the *Catechism* immediately shifts to discussions of Confession (CCC, 979-987). Confession is one of our strongest weapons in the fight against sin. It is one of the greatest gifts Christ gave to his Church (CCC, 981).

"There is no offense, however serious, that the Church cannot forgive…Christ who died for all men desires that in his Church the gates of forgiveness should always be open to anyone who turns away from sin (CCC, 982)." This is one of the most comforting paragraphs in the whole *Catechism*. Its point is clear: *Jesus is bigger than sin.* There is nothing we could ever do that Christ would be unable to heal and forgive. He reigns supreme; he is sovereign. May we never leave his loving, empowering, and all protecting side…and may we never doubt his ability to restore us to grace when we fall.

Is There Such a Thing as the "Unforgivable Sin"?

"But wait a minute," you may object, "doesn't the Bible talk about an 'unforgivable sin' somewhere?" Yes, it does. In fact, we learn about the "unforgivable sin" from the lips of Jesus himself. "Therefore I tell you, every sin and blasphemy will be forgiven men, but the blasphemy against the Spirit will not be forgiven (Matthew 12:31; Mark 3:29; Luke 12:10)" This can be a confusing passage, and there are some people who believe that they have somehow committed this "unforgivable sin." More often than not, however, these people haven't committed this sin and are just very confused about what, exactly, blasphemy against the Holy Spirit really is.

The *Catechism* offers some clarity on this troubling issue. It says that "there are no limits to the mercy of God, but anyone who deliberately refuses to accept his mercy by repenting, rejects the forgiveness of his sins and the salvation offered by the Holy Spirit. Such hardness of heart can lead to final impenitence and eternal loss (CCC, 1864)." The unforgivable sin is the refusal to repent of our sins and receive God's forgiveness. We cannot commit the unforgivable sin through a word or statement. We only commit the unforgivable sin when we actively and definitively refuse the offer of God's grace and mercy.

The late, great Pope John Paul II hammered this point home by saying that "'blasphemy' does not properly consist in offending against the Holy Spirit in words; it consists rather *in the refusal to accept the salvation which God offers to man through the Holy Spirit,* working through the power of the Cross." Jesus is constantly offering his love and mercy to us through the Holy Spirit, and "the blasphemy against the Holy Spirit consists precisely in the radical refusal to accept this forgiveness."[8]

In short, the only "unforgivable sin" is deliberately and finally rejecting God's forgiveness. He does not force his grace and mercy on anyone. It has to be freely embraced. And any person who sincerely asks for mercy will be forgiven.

Thus, if you're worried that you've committed the unforgivable sin, don't be. You haven't. If you *had* committed the unforgivable sin you won't be worried about it in the slightest. The very fact that you are concerned about the eternal state of your soul and want to receive mercy and forgiveness is proof that you haven't committed blasphemy against the Holy Spirit. Remember: our God is a God of infinite mercy. He is a Heavenly Father who will never withhold his mercy from a repentant person. If you sincerely ask for mercy and seek forgiveness, *you will get it.*

St. Paul experienced God's boundless mercy firsthand. Prior to his conversion, St. Paul was one of the most dangerous men of his time: he killed Christians. The Bible tells us that he had breathed "threats of murder against the disciples of the Lord (Acts 9:1)." Devoted to the persecutions of Christ's followers, Paul gave active consent to the brutal stoning of St. Stephen (Acts 7:54-8:1).

As unspeakable as his sins were, however, God was able to forgive Paul and restore him to grace and truth. And not only was he able to forgive St. Paul, God turned him into one of the most important saints in the history of the Church. In spite of his evils acts, God said that St. Paul would be "a chosen instrument of mine to carry my name before the Gentiles and kings and sons of Israel (Acts 9:15)." St. Paul's life witnesses to the fact that no sin is too great for God to forgive and no person too far gone for God to heal and transform.

How do I Know for Sure?

Several months ago I had a very memorable conversation with an old woman at a Catholic conference. She came up to me after one of my talks and introduced herself by saying that she was a regular at daily Mass, prayed the Rosary, and went to Confession on a regular basis. And before I could get a word in edgewise the woman went on to say something that caught me off guard.

"You know the thing about you I covet the most?" she asked.

I shook my head.

She leaned in, lowered her voice to a whisper, and said "I wish I had your certainty. I go to Mass and pray all the time, but deep down I still wonder whether all of this religious stuff is really as true and powerful as everyone says it is. I wish I had your faith and certainty."

And with that she disappeared into the crowd.

I share this story because I don't think this kindly old woman is unique — I think she's just unusually honest. A lot of us struggle with doubts about the things we believe. Many of us just accepted the Catholic Faith when we were young. We didn't know any better. We blindly took whatever our Dad or Mom or CCD teacher told us as fact.

However, as you grow older and begin to experience the world for yourselves, questions and doubts begin to arise. You start to think for yourself. You are less quick to take other people's word for things. You want evidence and proof to validate the claims people make. And now you look around the world and see a lot of pain and suffering, and somehow this doesn't seem to square with the Christian notion of a "good and powerful God." Mass is painfully boring and you wonder if it has any real meaning at all — *they say Jesus is in the Eucharist, but I don't see him… looks like a piece of circular cardboard to me.* These and a myriad of other questions begin to arise about the truth and reality of our Faith. And then, like the old woman, the doubts begin to grow within you…

Without a Doubt…

Again, I don't think this is uncommon or unusual. Every one of us asks, "How do I know if all of this Christian stuff is true?" at least once in our lives. Thus, if you've ever struggled with doubts about the Faith, take comfort in the fact that you're not alone. Some of Jesus' closest friends doubted him as well. We all know that story of "Doubting Thomas" who refused to believe that Jesus had really resurrected from the dead until he saw the risen Lord with his own eyes and placed his fingers and hands in Christ's wounds (John 20:24-29). Furthermore, the Gospel writers are honest about the fact that while most fell down and worshiped Jesus when they saw him after his resurrection, "some doubted" still (Matthew 28:17).

Doubt about Christ and the Faith is nothing new; it was present from the beginning. And while it is certainly not something to be desired, it is also not fatal to Christ or his Church. Jesus is bigger than our sins, struggles and doubts. He can take whatever challenges befall us and transform them into something glorious…if we let him.

Doubt is something we all face from time to time. And whenever doubt creeps up on us we need to remember two main things: First, it isn't the end of the world. Jesus didn't smite Thomas with a bolt of lightning for doubting, and he won't smite us either. Quite the contrary, our Lord went on to make "Doubting Thomas" a great saint and used him to proclaim the Gospel to great multitudes.

Jesus did this for St. Thomas and he can do the same thing for us as well.

Secondly, we need to remember that faith is a gift. We don't create it ourselves. If I am experiencing doubts about the sacred mysteries, no amount of grunting and straining is going to generate faith within me. I can't "force" myself to believe. The Bible is very clear that faith is something we receive…not create. When St. Peter made the earth-shattering announcement that Jesus was the Christ, Son of the living God, our Lord notes that "flesh and blood has not revealed this to you, but my Father who is in heaven (Matthew 16:17)." Peter didn't get his faith by solving a divine equation; his faith was a free gift from God. The *Catechism* also states that "before this faith can be exercised, man must have the grace of God to move and assist him; he must have the interior helps of the Holy Spirit, who moves the heart and converts it to God, who opens the eyes of the mind and makes it easy for all to accept and believe the truth (CCC, 153)."

Because faith is a gift, we must run to God whenever we experience doubt. We must be like the man who told Jesus "I believe; help my unbelief (Mark 9:24)." God wants to give us the gift of faith. He wants us to be able see the beauty of his divine truth and love. Thus, whenever you struggle with doubts, get down on your knees and ask him to remove any obstacles that prevent you from believing. Ask him to open your eyes to the fullness of truth. Ask him to give you the gift of faith…and rest assured that if you are sincere in your search and genuine in your request, God will certainly give you the eyes of faith.

Furthermore, it is important to remember that God is never bothered or offended by our questions. He wants us to learn more. He wants us to seek answers. As a young child learns by asking his parents questions like "how?" and "why?" so we as God's children learn by asking the same questions of our Heavenly Father. As long as we strive to find truth by trusting in the source of truth — God himself — we will be blessed immensely.

Truth is the key. We must never waver in our search for the real and the true. The challenge we face, however, is that some of the things which are most real and true are beyond our finite powers of understanding. And thus we must trust our Lord and Savior to guide us to those truths that are so grand we can't discern them on our own.

(Not) Surprised by Suffering

True happiness is only found in the love of Christ. The Lord is the source of lasting joy and solace. Jesus is the way, the truth, and the life (John 14:6). There is no real satisfaction and fulfillment apart from him. However, our Faith does *not* teach that the challenges of life magically disappear when we enter into a living relationship with Jesus. Christianity is hardly a ticket to heath and wealth; but it is certainly a means to real truth and true love.

Some people think that becoming a follower of Christ will solve all of our human problems. From every direction — television, Internet, radio — we are inundated with promises that this or that particular product will solve all of our problems. "Take this pill, and you will lose weight and be beautiful," "purchase this product, and your every need will be met," "read this book, and you will never have to study again." The world is a never ending factory of "quick fixes" for health, wealth, entertainment and friends. Why should faith and religion be any different? We've got drive-through restaurants, one-click ordering, and overnight shipping…why shouldn't our Faith offer instant gratification?

Although it would be nice, this isn't the Faith Christ gave us. Sadly, a lot of people come to our Savior expecting him to be the magical element that will give us health, wealth and earthly success. We expect God to be like a celestial Santa Claus who will give us all of the things we want. Jesus will make me beautiful, popular, and rich, right? Well, not necessarily. A life devoted to Christ is not a life of ease and comfort. The Christian life is hard. And the reason for this is simple: Jesus doesn't want to give us earthly comfort and human success…he wants to give us something infinite greater: *divine life and heavenly glory!* He wants us to be so united to him that every part of our life and being is transformed by his life and grace. This is radical. This is awesome. But it's not easy…if we truly follow Christ, we will experience pain and suffering from time to time.

As we've already seen, the sacrament of Baptism is the beginning of our life as God's children. "Do you not know that all of us who have been baptized into Christ Jesus were baptized into his death? We were buried therefore with him by Baptism into death, so that as Christ was raised from the dead by the glory of the Father, we too might walk in newness of life (Romans 6:3-4)." In Baptism we receive the fullness of grace. Yet, this life is not of some generic variety; it is nothing less than the life of Christ himself. He doesn't give us "some" life; he gives us his life. Through Baptism, we are incorporated into Christ and participate in his sonship. As creatures we live, move and have our being in him (Acts 17:28). As our sovereign Lord, he lives, moves and extends his being in us.

This is the power of Christ's love. It makes us divine children. He unites us to himself and transforms *what* we are into *who* he is. "Baptism not only purifies from all sins, but also makes the neophyte a 'new creature,' an adopted son of God, who has become a 'partaker of the divine nature,' a member of Christ and co-heir with him, and a temple of the Holy Spirit (CCC, 1265)." This is the Gospel. This is the grace we have been given. This is the life we are called to live. *We are sons and daughters of God.*

> "All who are led by the Spirit of God are sons of God… you have received the spirit of sonship. When we cry, 'Abba! Father!' it is the Spirit himself bearing witness with our spirit that we are children of God, and if children, then heirs, heirs of God and fellow heirs with Christ, *provided we suffer with him in order that we may also be glorified with him* (Romans 8:14-17, emphasis added)."

I had always loved Romans 8…at least, up until that last verse. This passage is perplexing. It surprises us. We tend to regard suffering as an indicator of divine displeasure. Suffering is something we expect when we have somehow offended the Almighty. It implies great distance between us and our Heavenly Father. And yet St. Paul seems to be saying the exact opposite of this. Not only does he say that it is okay to suffer; he seems to suggest that suffering with Christ is actually a *condition* for our glorification with Christ. *St. Paul says that suffering is something that we — as followers of Jesus — will, not might, experience.*

The Apostle goes on to ask: "Who shall separate us from the love of Christ? Shall tribulation, or distress, or persecution, or famine, or nakedness, or peril, or sword (Romans 8:35)?" While most of us would tend to respond with an emphatic "Yes!" St. Paul does not.

In fact, he suggests that suffering is one of the things that *unites* us even more fully to the person and work of our Lord. He states that far from separating us from the love of God "in all these things we are more than conquerors through him [Jesus] who loved us (Romans 8:37)." Suffering is not a sign of defeat. In it we find our victory. It is in the pain that we can encounter Jesus. This is why St. James instructed us to "count it all joy, my brethren, when you meet various trials, for you know that the testing of your faith produces steadfastness… that you may be perfect and complete, lacking in nothing (James 1:2-3)."

The world is a confusing place. Natural disasters, violence, physical ailments, and tragedies seem to plague our every step. And while we strive to trust in God's loving care and concern, there are moments in each of our lives when we want to stop, look up to heaven, raise our fist and ask: "How can you — the all-powerful, sovereign God — permit these things to happen? They say you're a God of love; where is the love in all of this?"

Although it is normal to raise such questions, we must remember that they are often without a human answer. "As the heavens are higher than the earth, so are my ways higher than your ways and my thoughts [higher] than your thoughts (Isaiah 55:9)." St. Paul understands our confusion, and he sympathizes with our struggles. However, he assures us that "in everything God works for good with those who love Him, who are called according to His purpose (Romans 8:28)." Remember: God is sovereign; He is in control. We may not know the particular reasons why God permits certain calamities to arise, but we do know that his loving care and concern remains constant throughout.

God sees more than we see. He loves more than we love. And He is working to bring about a greater good than we could have ever imagined (or accomplished) on our own.

Living His Life...Carrying His Cross

Everyone suffers; even saints and apostles. And while we don't always understand the meaning or purpose behind suffering, St. Paul tells us how we ought to respond when suffering hits. "I rejoice in my sufferings for your sake, and in my flesh I complete what is lacking in Christ's afflictions for the sake of his body, that is, the church (Colossians 1:24)."

Wow! This statement almost sounds crazy! Not only does St. Paul say that he rejoices in his suffering (something that is utterly bizarre — why would anyone *rejoice* in suffering?), but the Apostle also states that he makes up for what is "lacking" in the afflictions of Christ. This is shocking. How can Christ lack anything? He's God, after all...isn't God's love infinite?

Jesus' love is indeed infinite. In and of itself it lacks nothing. The "lack" is not located in Jesus. It is located in us. Through our Baptism we enter into the life of Christ — *every* part of it. Suffering included. Jesus didn't suffer and die so that we don't have to. He suffered and died so that *our* suffering and death (which we can't escape) could be a means to his life.

Suffering is difficult. No one enjoys it. But following Christ means carrying his Cross. And the Cross is the ultimate sign of this truth and love.

St. Josemaría Escrivá said it well: "You ask me if I had a Cross to bear. And I answered: 'Yes, we always have to bear the Cross'. But it is a glorious Cross, a divine seal, the authentic guarantee of being children of God. That is why, with the Cross, we always travel happily on our way."[9]

We are not alone in the many struggles we face in life. Christ was "made like his brethren in every respect," and he "has suffered and been tempted, he is able to help those who are tempted (Hebrews 2:18)." We have a loving Savior who can identify with our struggles. He knows the trials we face. We are not alone. "For as we share abundantly in Christ's sufferings, so through Christ we share abundantly in comfort too (2 Corinthians 1:5)." Our Lord loves us. And he will never leave nor forsake us —"he comforts us in all our afflictions (2 Corinthians 1:4)."

Our Faith is a Faith of power and love. It enables us to face all of the struggles of life with and in the life of Christ himself. Trials are real. Difficulties abound. But the grace of our Lord is even more real and even more present.

Jesus loved so that we could love. Jesus gave himself so that we could receive him. He stoops to our level so that we might be raised to his. He is with us in our tears so that we can be with him in his joys. This is his love. This is our faith.

Christ will see us through the hard times. And he won't let go until he has fully situated us with him in the glory of heaven.

You Call this "Good News"???

Okay, okay, okay…we've been covering a lot of spiritually explosive ground in this chapter, and I'm sure there are a few of you who are a little freaked out by some of the things we have been discovering in the writings of St. Paul. Some of you may be thinking to yourself, "I thought this book was going to help me feel good about things…but right now I'm just overwhelmed by all this talk about sin, temptation, and suffering." Some of you may even be discouraged, thinking, "This Christian stuff is harder than I expected… maybe it's harder than it's worth."

We understand your feelings. But hold up just a couple of seconds so we can clarify a few things. First, Christianity isn't a walk-in-the-park religion — it's a *radical Faith*. One of the great tragedies of our modern period is that so many of us have forgotten just how radical a lifestyle Christianity demands of its followers. Pope Benedict XVI has made this point very clear as well. In his first papal encyclical, *Deus Caritas Est* ("God is Love"), the Holy Father said that we're called to embrace a life of love "in its most radical form." By contemplating the radical love of Jesus on the Cross "the Christian discovers the path along which his life and love must move" (*Deus Caritas Est*, section 12).

This lifestyle of radical love is something we may have forgotten, but fortunately this is something that St. Paul never forgot.

Our Faith has to be at the center of everything we do. It has to be at the very center of *who we are*. Love for Jesus Christ needs to be the motivation for our every thought, word, and deed. This "Christ-centeredness" was so important to St. Paul that he decided "to know nothing among you except Jesus Christ and him crucified (1 Corinthians 2:2)." He held nothing back, giving everything to Jesus and his Church: "I do not account my life of any value nor as precious to myself, if only I may accomplish my course and the ministry which I received from the Lord Jesus, to testify to the Gospel of the grace of God (Acts 20:24)." This may sound crazy to some of us, but it made perfect sense to St. Paul because nothing else carries ultimate significance except the person and work of Jesus on the Cross (Galatians 6:14).

"For to me to live is Christ, to die is gain (Philippians 1:20-21)." St. Paul treasured his relationship with Jesus above everything and said that he "count[ed] everything as loss because of the surpassing worth of knowing Christ Jesus my Lord (Philippians 3:7-8)." The Apostle showed us what it means to rely completely on God in times of difficulty (2 Corinthians 1:8-9), and he reminded us that nothing can compare with the joy and happiness awaiting us in heaven (2 Corinthians 4:16-17).

The point in all of this is simple: Christ is great! And he wants to free us from this culture of sin and death and lead us to the glories of his Heavenly Kingdom. That's not an easy journey. Being a child of God can be hard at times, but we shouldn't get discouraged. Discouragement and despair are two of Satan's greatest weapons. The Devil knows how powerful Christ is. He knows what a beautiful plan God has for your life. And the last thing the devil wants is for you to find your strength in Christ. His greatest nightmare is your joy in Jesus.

Thus, Satan will do everything in his power to discourage you from following Christ. He will remind you of all your sins, weaknesses and shortcomings. He will try to get you to believe that you are just too far gone for God to save. Whenever you have these thoughts and feelings, immediately get down on your knees in prayer and remind yourself that there is *no* sin that God can't forgive, and that there is no person God doesn't love with a burning passion. Don't let shame and guilt keep you from Christ. Jesus can overcome everything and use anything to bring about his glory.

In fact, it is often in our weaknesses that we encounter the God's strength (2 Corinthians 12:8-10).

Be Not Afraid!

Another tactic that Satan employs in the battle for souls is *fear*. Fear is a subtle thing, and it can take various forms. A lot of us are afraid to face our sinful past and admit that we are sinners in desperate need of a savior. We run from ourselves and do everything we can to drown out the truth about who we are and what we've done. I am convinced that this kind of fear is one of the main reasons why addictions are so prevalent in our contemporary culture. We are terrified to face our true selves, and we try to lose ourselves in drugs, alcohol, sex, pornography, television and the Internet — anything to take our minds off of our miserable reality.

This is tragic. We need not be afraid. God is sovereign. He knows everything — from the worst thing you've ever done, to the greatest thing you'll ever do. There are no surprises to our Heavenly Father. He won't run away from our true selves, and neither should we. Instead, we should turn to Jesus, admit our shortcomings and failures, and ask him to do the thing he desires most: to heal us from our wounds and transform us by his grace.

There is nothing — no sin, evil, crime — that God can't overcome, there is not wound that He can't heal, and there is no person He will turn away. God is love. And He loves you more than you could ever know.

One of the reasons why people hesitate to give themselves completely to Jesus is because they are afraid of change. We are creatures of comfort and routine. We have pretty nice lives. Granted, things could be a little better, and we see the advantages to following Christ, but we'd much rather stay put than make any modifications to our lives.

This type of fear is unfounded as well. There are times when radical change is necessary. We need to reject anything that prevents us from embracing the fullness of Christ's love. Sometimes that means making some pretty drastic modifications to our lifestyles. For some of us that might mean burning those hidden magazines, getting an Internet filter, chucking those DVDs and CDs, or finding a new group of friends to hang out with. None of these things are easy, but there are times when we need to make some radical changes so that our life can be more centered on Christ and open to his grace.

I Surrender All

To most of us, the word "surrender" carries a negative connotation. We associate it with defeat. "Surrendering" is something you do when you have no other options; when you lose. In the world's eyes, surrendering is a sign of weakness.

Not so for the Christian. In fact, far from being a sign of loss or defeat, surrendering is the way we arrive at sure victory and success. When I surrender to God's sovereign plan for my life, He is able to bless me in ways that I couldn't even begin to imagine. All of us are afraid to trust God. We're afraid that He won't know how to make us truly happy. We would much rather make our own plans and decisions and leave God out of it.

Ironic as it is, however, we will only find true happiness if we submit to the plan of God. We will only have victory if we surrender to His loving guidance. St. Paul was adamant about this point: "We know that in everything God works for good with those who love him, who are called according to his purpose (Romans 8)." Every part of God's plan is ordered to our lasting joy and happiness. He wants you to be happy more than you want to be happy. He wants you to find joy more than you want to find joy. And He is able to give you a delight and pleasure the likes of which no human mind has ever envisioned.

God is a sovereign Father. He is almighty over all, but His power is rooted in His fatherly love. We need to love Him completely, give ourselves totally to Him, and entrust all that we have to the care of His perfect, loving plan.

God has a plan for your life. Surrender your life to Him, and you will find your eternal victory.

Find Yourself in Christ

Surrendering your life to Jesus can be a difficult thing to do. Some of us aren't even sure who we really are and why we're here. Every person is searching for the meaning of life. We are all trying to figure out our purpose, our worth, our identity. Each year dozens of self-help books are written promising their readers answers and "tips and tricks" on how to wade through life and discover the answers we all seek.

Whether we realize it or not, Jesus Christ is the answer to all of our questions. His love is the only thing that can get us through the hard times. His healing touch is the only thing that can restore us when we fall. His mercy is the only thing that can pull us out of sin and weakness. And, his grace is the only thing that can provide the eternal happiness we so desperately seek.

I'd be lying if I said that life — the Christian life, in particular — is easy. It's not. It's the hardest thing we'll ever have to face. However, the Christian life is also the only thing that can give joy to the sad, strength to the weak, healing to the wounded and victory to the defeated. God loved us so much that He sent his only Son into the world so that we might be liberated from slavery to sin and given the joys of heaven (Romans 6:17-23). This is the Gospel. This is our strength. This is our Faith. And may we join St. Paul in living our every day in the life and love of our Beautiful Savior: "For me to live is Christ, and to die is gain (Philippians 1:21)."

CHAPTER FIVE

MAKE SPACE FOR CHRIST:
HOW MAN RELATES TO ONE ANOTHER

I received a letter the other day. No not an e-mail — a letter. It struck me as odd. When I opened my mailbox, an actual mailbox, and retrieved the envelope (yes, an actual paper, sealed, stamped envelope) it hit me that I haven't received a letter in years. I receive bills and ads, magazines and Christmas cards. I receive plenty of correspondence from people asking me for money (though I have none), but a letter…this hadn't happened in quite some time.

I actually got excited. I ripped it open and found several pages, handwritten. Much to my dismay, I came to a disappointing conclusion as I began reading it. I had no idea who the person was who had written the letter. The handwriting was unfamiliar, the greeting was odd and the story on the opening page mentioned people and situations I knew nothing about.

I turned over the envelope and quickly realized that the letter was not addressed to me. Apparently, our postal worker isn't used to handling letters very much, either, as he put someone else's letter in our box. At once, my balloon of joy popped. I now had to carefully refold and surgically re-tape the envelope, writing a letter of apology on it to its rightful owner, to make up for my overzealous though unintentional felony of opening their mail.

It did strike me, though, just how media-driven and technologically inundated I (and we as a culture) had become. I couldn't even recall the last time I had received a paper letter and hadn't felt that feeling of joy in receiving a letter in years. The more I thought about it, most of my communication had been replaced by the phone several years ago…then e-mail, then text messaging.

In fact, if someone were to ask, "How does man relate to others?" the most popular answer nowadays would probably be MySpace (followed by Facebook as a close second).

Can you imagine what far-reaching, global evangelization St. Paul could have done with the Internet? St. Paul would have liked the Internet, seeing in it an inexhaustible tool for spreading the Gospel. What would quickly reveal itself to him, however, is how this tool for potential good can so quickly and easily be manipulated for evil (Romans 7:21), as well.

This apostle, this saint, constantly challenged the culture of the day, urging man to die to self and sacrifice personally for the good of the Church. He would have liked the intention behind social networking and virtual communities like MySpace or Facebook, but also would have seen their potential to become an obstacle to true Christian community. Now, before any MySpace lovers reading this get offended, it's important to make two things clear. First of all, Internet communities like MySpace are not intrinsically evil, they, like anything on earth, can be used for good or evil. The choice is in the hands (and hearts) of those posting and reading. That being said, it's vital for everyone in today's online communities to answer the following questions: "Are my actions, words, pictures and profile glorifying God, my Savior? Does my page or do my postings reflect my focus on God or on myself? Am I an arrow pointing *others* to God or to myself?" If the answers to these questions are not God-focused than, odds are, we're wasting an incredible opportunity to share His love with others.

This chapter is about how man (you and me and everyone) relates to others. The point is not to condemn MySpace, it is just one example of a much larger struggle we have as the children of God — the struggle is one of authenticity and for true community.

Two Versions of Self

How many people know the *real* you? Not, the "you" that you portray to the world, but the true, authentic you, in all of your bratty-ness, moodiness, selfishness, ego and pride?

Wow, that's not a fun way to begin a chapter, now is it? We have to start here, though, if we really want to understand where St. Paul wants to lead us. Even if you don't utilize MySpace or Facebook, the truths and themes we're discussing here are easily transferable to any and all relationships you currently have, so keep reading.

Remember back in Chapter Three, when we talked about self-awareness? It's important to recognize that self-awareness isn't just awareness of oneself but also an awareness of how others view that self. Online communities like MySpace are engaging and dynamic and also very telling. Peoples' profiles usually demonstrate two distinctly different things: how people *want* to be seen and, as a result, how people *are actually* seen.

Man often has two versions of himself.

The first version is the person seen by most of the world, the person we try to portray in our conversation, dress, attitude and personality (like on MySpace pages). People use backgrounds, music, text and pictures to communicate things about themselves to all who visit their page(s). People take provocative photographs in suggestive poses. Biographies tell the world what we want them to know about us — everything from our current mood to our latest thoughts and favorite books (that we haven't finished), to what television and films are currently forming our daily morality. Many of the pages proudly portray "images" of ourselves that we want others to consider authentic displays of our innermost beings. What is interesting is that most viewers mock others' profiles as insincere, inauthentic or outright laughable, without ever stopping to think that someone might be doing the same thing to their own profile. Version one is a "self-portrait."

The second version is the one that comes out in real life, and usually only around the ones you love and live with. The second version is the "real" you, the one that rears its early morning "bedhead" for only a select few to see. It's the version of you when the makeup is off, the pajamas are on, the hair isn't combed and you're surrounded only by those who are "legally obligated" to love you. Would the people who see *this* version of you say that the MySpace profile or "self-portrait" is an accurate assessment of who you are? An even deeper question would be, "Would *God* look at your MySpace profile and rejoice, because it represented all He hopes for you to be (Jeremiah 29:11, Ephesians 2:10)?" Beyond MySpace, would God look at your relationships at school, work and home, and thank you for putting His truth and His will ahead of your wants? Do you relate to others with a Godly perspective?

Modern media gurus say that handheld devices and the Internet have revolutionized the way we communicate with and relate to one another. St. Paul would offer a different answer. Technology is fine, he would say but, when asked how man relates to others, Paul would offer just one word for his answer: "Love."

If you say, "That's a nice idea, but that's not how it is," you could have lived in Rome a couple of thousand years ago. It was to hardened hearts like ours that St. Paul wrote. For Paul, truly loving one another was not some "fairy tale fantasy." It was achievable, but with a catch: it has to start with you, not someone else. It's easy to say, "I love you" with your words, but true love isn't about words, it's about actions.

Jesus showed us (and Paul reminds us) that our actions will always, ultimately, be motivated by the absence or presence of one thing: love.

True Love is the Answer

> "I was there when they crucified my Lord
> I held the scabbard when the soldier drew his sword
> I threw the dice when they pierced his side
> But I've seen love conquer the great divide"
>
> — "When Love Comes to Town", U2 and B.B. King

Have you ever seen the crucifixion of your Savior? Not in a movie, but in your own heart, in prayer? Have you ever truly pictured Golgotha, where Christ was executed for you?

Try to picture it now. When the earthquake subsided and the darkness lifted that Friday afternoon, it must have resembled something of a crime scene. Ask the Holy Spirit to guide your mind and heart now as you discern the site.

Survey the rocky ground. Feel the stones crushing one another and moving beneath your feet. Hear the eerie wind whistle through the valley below muffling the sobbing of your Mother. See the blood stained rocks and cloths that surround the site. Notice the indifference of the guards on duty. Hear the mockery and gossip of the remaining onlookers. Ask yourself why anyone would perform such an unspeakable act upon another human being, much less allow such an act when he had the power to stop it instantly.

Now, look forward to where the wood enters the stony ground. Let your eyes slowly track up the blood-stained wood. See the spike driven through the feet. Witness the flesh hanging from the bones like ribbons. Look at the nails in His hands, the hands that washed feet and broke the bread. Look upon your savior, again, for the first time.

On Good Friday, love conquered the great divide between God and man and between God's children.

Man relates to others, to one another, in the same way in which God relates to man…through love. Mankind comes together in times of suffering but, ultimately, what brings people together, even more than mutual suffering, is sacrificial love. Love conquers the greatest divides of hatred, racism, greed, lust, sexism, etc., but it doesn't stop there — love conquers sin and love destroys death. That is how Christ defeated Satan, not merely with the blood of sacrifice, but with the blood, sweat and tears of love.

How can such a gruesome sight simultaneously be so beautiful? The answer is this: love. It was because of the love involved.

Love Requires Bodily Sacrifice

You're going to find in this chapter that love is the answer. I don't mean that figuratively, but literally. To almost every question asked, the answer will be "love," because, to Paul, love was the answer to every question (re-read 1 Corinthians 13).

When St. Paul envisioned the cross of Christ, he saw in Jesus what our Heavenly Father sees…perfect love. St. Paul must have had the crucifix engrained in his mind and emblazoned on his heart when he penned the following words to the Romans:

> "I appeal to you, therefore, brethren, by the mercies of God, to present your bodies as a living sacrifice, holy and acceptable to God, which is your spiritual worship (Romans 12:1)."

Offering our bodies as a sacrifice can be looked at in two ways. The first way involves the "do not's", as in do not have premarital sex, do not look at pornography, do not use profanity, do not be lustful, do not abuse your bodies with drugs or alcohol. These are obvious sins and St. Paul definitely would have included all of them (and many more) in what we ought to sacrifice. True sacrifice like the kind mentioned in this verse, however, goes even deeper into the "do's", as well, as in what Christians *should* do with their bodies. We should pray, serve others, work for justice, remain pure, affirm others, live the virtues, etc. This verse is simultaneously telling us to "put to death" the deeds of the flesh (Romans 8:13) and to be righteous (Romans 6:13).

St. Paul is telling us to be countercultural. Most in the world put themselves first. He is calling us to change our attitudes and free our minds with the Gospel message, to reject worldliness and selfishness.

> "Do not be conformed to this world but be transformed by the renewal of your mind, that you may prove what is the will of God, what is good and acceptable and perfect (Romans 12:2)."

St. Paul warns us about people who twist the truth (Romans 1:18-32, 2 Timothy 4:1-6). Modern "wannabe" philosophers claim to have truth but offer little more than self. God's will must guide us in all circumstances, otherwise it is "*my* will be done," which was Adam's sin. Living like Christ, the new Adam, means we seek God's will and *that* is how we are transformed into God's image (Romans 8:29, 2 Corinthians 3:28), how we become "good and acceptable and perfect."

Christ's identity and kingship were not made known by the sign above his head which proclaimed his "title." Christ's identity upon that wood was made known by the beautiful and mangled body that hung beneath the placard. Words didn't proclaim the kingship of Jesus, the sacrifice of His body did. It's not the sign on the parish you attend that makes you a Catholic. It's not the words on a t-shirt, the message on the bumper sticker, the Rosary around the rearview or the title on the parochial uniform that makes you a Catholic.

It's what you do with your body (and what you don't do) that makes you a true Catholic, a true Christian. St. Paul understood this fact and lived it out with the core of his being. We can learn a lot from him.

That is what the body of Christ does…it dies, out of love, in order to rise and bring life. Why did Christ die? The answer is this: love.

There is No "I" in T-E-A-M (but there are three in humiliation)

We were humiliated by the loss. Hundreds of hours of training, countless days icing sore joints and heating muscles, and all the eight of us had to show for it was a last-place finish. It was a difficult way to learn an important lesson. I had made our collegiate crew team several months earlier, though I had never rowed in a boat before, much less rowed competitively. I quickly learned how difficult a sport it was to master.

I had begun training in an eight-man boat, with the other novices. Our coach, called a coxswain, was amazed at how a few of us had gelled and adapted so quickly. Not long after, four of us who (apparently) showed promise were moved to our own, smaller shell (boat). We immediately excelled. Our movements were synchronized. We were four bodies functioning as one and we won, a lot — so much so, that when we were asked to rejoin the eight-man shell for a race, we were convinced that we could turn the other four rowers into champions, like we had become. To quote Scripture, as St. Paul often did, "pride (went) before destruction (Proverbs 16:18)."

We had grown so comfortable with just our team of four that we didn't bother to adapt or to include the other quartet in "our" race. We were favored to win. Instead we came in dead last. Twice our shell stalled, once almost capsizing, because our eight oars were not functioning in unison. The blades were not at the same angles. The strokes were not at the same speeds. Put simply, we were "one" in name only, but our team was not a true team at all. Had we taken advantage of one another's gifts, talents and individual skill sets, we assuredly would have won. We failed not because we lost; we failed because of pride. We had the individual talent but not the unity.

One Body, Filled with Gifts

I wish St. Paul could have been the coxswain of our crew team. He would have coached us and guided us with the wisdom of Christ, like he offered those in Rome. "Do not think of (yourself) more highly than you ought" (Romans 12:3), he would have warned us. "You all have gifts that differ, according to God's grace," (Romans 12:6) Paul would have reminded.

Our gifts and talents are just that — gifts — that come from God's grace. The Greek word for grace is *charis*, which is the root word for "gift" (*charismata*). Incidentally, that is why the spiritual gifts of tongues or prophecy or teaching/ preaching are considered "charismatic" gifts. The term "charismatic" doesn't just refer to a movement or a "style" of prayer, it literally means gift.

Paul offers a quick overview of some of the spiritual *gifts* in Romans 12:4-8, and a far more in-depth examination of them in 1 Corinthians 12. It is worth a prayerful read. Understanding the spiritual gifts and the mystical body of Christ necessitates more than a pragmatic, logical approach — it requires a prayerful discernment of the heart, including discernment of your own spiritual gifts, which you may have yet to really tap into. Spiritual gifts are like muscles: if they're not used, they atrophy. God endows us all with gifts; He gives them freely but with expectation for use. Like any family we are expected by our Father to share.

Children Share, Brats Don't

"I am only one, but I am one.
 I can't do everything, but I can do something.
 And what I can do, I ought to do.
 And what I ought to do, by the grace of God, I shall do."

—Edward Everett Hale

God's hope and, frankly, His expectation is that "as each has received a gift, (that we would) employ it for one another, as good stewards of God's varied grace (1 Peter 4:10)." Seeing the link between God's grace and our gifts is vital because Paul wants us to remember that everything comes from God. The only thing in this world that is all ours is our sin. Everything else is a gift from God, our Father.

I could have said to Paul, "But I really worked hard at crew. I woke up every morning at 4 a.m., I ran six miles a day, and rowed for three hours a day. We didn't just win because of God-given athletic ability but because of hard work". Paul would smirk, shake his disbelieving head and remind me that *even my work ethic* is a gift from God. God doesn't give people gifts that He doesn't want them to use for His glory. So, as Paul said, "let us use them" (Romans 12:6). We should use God's gifts, constantly, for His glory not our own.

"In doing what we ought, we deserve no praise, because it is our duty."
— St. Augustine

As a good Coach, though, he wouldn't have stopped there. He would want to be sure that we understood why we failed to achieve our goal of victory and why we failed to "finish the race" (1 Corinthians 9:24, 2 Timothy 4:7). We functioned singularly, we focused more on the "I" than on the "we," and that's not Christian.

> "For as in one body we have many members, and all the members do not have the same function, so we, though many, are one body in Christ, and individually members one of another… (Romans 12:4)"

As sons and daughters of Christ, which indeed we are as we discussed in Chapter Two, we belong to one another. Like the "old-school" Christmas lights on a strand, if one bulb burns out the rest of the strand is useless, it cannot achieve its purpose or function. We are all connected in the mystical body of Christ; we need one another. In fact, it's God's will that we need one another (CCC 1937).

Christ taught us this principle in the parable of the talents (Matthew 25). God gives different measures of gifts to different people, so that we would work together and rely upon one another in love. Our gifts are complimentary, that is to say, they only see their fullest potential when used in conjunction with others' gifts.

We form and build this one body when we share not only our material goods or our personal talents, but when we share our *spiritual gifts,* as well. The Church teaches about this when she speaks of "solidarity". Simply put, solidarity can be thought of as "all for one and one for all…for a specific goal." Far more deeply, the Church tells us that solidarity is "an eminently Christian virtue (CCC 1948)."

What the Church is telling us is that for us to live a truly virtuous life, we must not only "have concern" for others, we must actively work for one another's salvation (1 Peter 1:9). For we, as believers, to become all that God designed us to become, we must see our faith walk as being connected to every one else's faith walks and, next, *do something about it*. Solidarity is shown through sharing not only our material gifts but also in the sharing of our spiritual gifts, in sacrificing for others.

And *why* do we sacrifice for others? Why do we offer our gifts in service to our brothers and sisters? The answer is this: love.

It's Social Justice, not Social "Just Us"

"All that is necessary for the triumph of evil is that good men do nothing."
— Edmund Burke

How would you feel if you worked hard in your job each day, only to have your paycheck withheld from you? You would be upset, to say the least. How about if you had your home taken from you without reason? What would you do if you didn't have enough money to feed yourself or your children? Would you resort to a life of crime? Would you strike back at those who were unjust toward you? What if you desperately needed help from others but you were turned away because of your religion or your skin color or your age? What if you had no voice and "no right to speak?" What if you were denied your right to worship freely? What if someone else, someone in worldly authority, decided to "rescind" your right to live? What if your life wasn't worth much in the eyes and mind and "philosophy" of another? That would not be justice and that is not of God.

We receive our human dignity from God, as we are created in His image. Man, all mankind, is endowed with *transcendent dignity*. Now, what does that mean, exactly?

Transcendent means that it "comes from beyond our normal, physical human experience". In other words, life doesn't just come from a man and woman having sex, but from the man, the woman *and God.*

Dignity means "the inherent and unchanging value of a person, created in God's own image and likeness." In other words, our worth comes not from what "we do or offer society," but our worth comes from He whom we came from.

So, we (you and I) are endowed with a worth that is beyond this world, that cannot and should not be destroyed by this world, for all life ultimately came, comes and will come only from God.

Paul didn't offer these teachings as "philosophy" like many of his Greek contemporaries might have done. No, for Paul, justice and solidarity were inseparably linked with true Christian living; Paul didn't look at service or justice as theoretical, but very practical.

> "We, though many, are one body in Christ, and individually members of one another. Having gifts that differ according to the grace given to us, **let us use them** (Romans 12:5-6, emphasis added)…"

God freely gives us His grace and so, we ought, freely give our gifts and put them at the service of others (1 Peter 4:10), especially those most in need. *The Catechism of the Catholic Church* sums it up beautifully, saying, "The duty of making oneself a neighbor to others and actively serving them becomes even more urgent when it involves the disadvantaged (CCC 1932)…" This is what it means when Christ says, "whatever you do to the least of my brothers, you do to me (Matthew 25:40)." Take the time and immerse yourself in the Church's wisdom on this subject (CCC 1928-1948).

It's been said that love is blind; justice is supposed to be blind, as well. Many modern day Christians, including Catholics, often times will try to pick and choose the Gospel elements they wish to follow. Some will speak out intently and passionately about the "immigration debate" but remain silent regarding abortion. Others will pray Rosaries outside abortion clinics but quickly dismiss the alien, the outcast, the refugee or those of other cultures or ethnicities most in need of humanitarian aid and relief. St. Paul is very intentional in the way he advocates for Christians to look out for one another, and to serve one another in mutual affection. He reminded the folks in Ephesus that "the work of ministry (is) building up the body of Christ (Ephesians 4:12)."

True Christians, as Paul notes, must embrace the entire Gospel of life, the Gospel of life that our Roman Catholic Church upholds in the face of all obstacles, political, social and physical.

How can you best love Christ? Seek justice.

How can you best love all of mankind? Seek Christ.

How can you embrace the *entire* Gospel of life? The answer is this: with love.

Communion Isn't Just a Sunday Thing

Solidarity requires communion. Justice requires communion. So now the only question is, "What is communion, exactly?"

When you hear the word "communion" you probably think of rising from your pew during Mass and walking forward to receive the Eucharist. Certainly, that is Communion. In truth, though, communion *is that and a whole lot more*. It's not just the "action" of going forward to receive Jesus in His precious Body and Blood, true communion means becoming *one with* God.

The dictionary defines communion as "an exchange of intimate thoughts and feelings." And while the good folks at Webster do a nice job, that isn't nearly deep enough. Communion in Christ is more than "sharing common feelings" and more than expressing "intimate feelings." The Christian life is about learning how to surrender to God, it is a gift of self. True communion (in Christ) is giving yourself back to God *and to* His children, mankind.

It is the Holy Spirit who brings us into communion with Christ. St. Paul tells us that it is only by the Holy Spirit that we can even proclaim that Christ is Lord (1 Corinthians 12:3)! The same way that Christ leads us into a more intimate relationship (and exchange of self) with God the Father, the Holy Spirit leads us into a more intimate relationship with Christ.

In addition, we are called to be in communion not only with Christ, but with His greater body, the Church. The Latin root word for communion, *communio*, means "common;" we are bound together with the greater body of Christ, a body of believers with whom we have *common* beliefs and share *common* realities. One of the "realities" that we share is that God is God and we are not; God is the Creator, we are His creation.

At Holy Mass we come together, in community (same root word), and enter into physical and spiritual communion with one another and with God. At that same time, we are surrounded by all of the saints and angels (Hebrews 12:1), in *communion* with the mystical body of Christ (the *Communion* of Saints) who have gone before us. In God's timelessness, we are worshipping alongside the heavenly host (saints and angels), during this re-presentation of Christ's once-and-for-all perfect sacrifice, in perfect communion. Then, during the Mass, we receive Communion (Christ's true presence) in order that we might become saints ourselves!

"One Body" Through Him, With Him, In Him

The Holy Mass is a celebration of Christ's sacrifice to the Father. It is taking place every moment of every day (except on Good Friday) in some corner of the world. Masses have been offered and celebrated on land and sea and in the air. The Mass has taken place on battlefields and in castles, in prisons and in jungles, in stadiums and in catacombs. Thousands of times every Sunday throughout the world, we hear the same readings and the same words of consecration.

Catholics are united and bound by this sacrifice, the one True Meal that surpasses time, geography, language, class and race. At the Eucharistic table of our Lord, we become one body, as we become one with His Body.

The Holy Mass is a liturgy, two liturgies, actually — the Liturgy of the Word, and the Liturgy of the Eucharist. Liturgy is "a public work, done in the service of another," that means we don't only go to receive, but to give. The common misconception is that we "go to Mass" only to receive Jesus in the Scriptures (Word) and in His flesh and blood (Eucharist). While that is true, that is not the sole purpose of going to Mass. You are at Mass to offer your witness and your love. You are there for the people sitting around you, those experiencing the highs and the lows that come with a life lived for Christ. In offering your body and your presence, you follow the example of Christ, who is truly, physically present under the appearance of bread and wine.

> "The cup of blessing…is it not a participation in the blood of Christ?
> The bread which we break, is it not a participation in the body of Christ?
> Because there is one bread, we who are many are one body, for we all
> partake of one bread (1 Corinthians 10:16-17)."

St. Paul absolutely believed in Christ's true presence in the Eucharist, which we will go into in more detail later. What is vital to understand, is that for St. Paul, we are not just called to be "emotionally" united to one another, but physically united, as well. At no time is the body of Christ more connected or more "one" than when we are at Catholic Mass. Of course, that doesn't mean that we won't have conflicts; every family has controversy. We even offer a time in Mass for reconciliation with our brothers and sisters in the body of believers, during the kiss (sign) of peace. What should this teach us?

How ought we handle controversy within the One Body of Christ? That's right…with love.

Family Feud – Dealing with Controversy

Sometimes people mistakenly believe that to be "Christian" means never arguing and disagreeing. Nothing could be farther from the truth. Our Lord Himself warned us to anticipate disagreements. Living as a Christian doesn't mean that we shouldn't ever disagree, but it means that we need to learn how to disagree respectfully and "argue with love." Ask yourself this question: "When I argue with people, is it out of a desire to get them to hear me or to *get them to Heaven?*" If it's not the latter, it's not worth the argument, because it's not of God.

To constantly and consistently love others, even those we disagree with or have a conflict with, is how we "outdo one another in showing honor" as St. Paul directs us to do (Romans 12:10). Listen, again, to his advice to the Christians in Colossae, regarding the need to live in peace and to seek love:

> "Put on then, as God's chosen ones, holy and beloved, compassion,
> kindness, lowliness, meekness and patience, forbearing one another and,
> if one has a complaint against another, forgiving each other; as the Lord
> has forgiven you, so you must also forgive. And over all these put on love,
> which binds everything together in perfect harmony (Colossians 3:12-14)."

Did you catch what St. Paul said "binds everything together in perfect harmony?" The answer is this: love.

Compassion and kindness, meekness and patience all require love and love requires living in the truth. Some modern "Christians" employ the "Well, I wouldn't do it, but I'm not going to tell someone else how to live their life" excuse. St. Paul would have much stronger words. He'd warn us about casting judgment (Romans 14), yes, but he'd warn us even more sternly about being so careless about others' sins…in doing so, we show we "care less" about their souls.

Not correcting our brothers and sisters who are in sin is a sin of omission, a sin against the greater body of Christ. Jesus was quite clear when He commanded us "Take heed to yourselves; if your brother sins, rebuke him, and if he repents, forgive him…(Luke 17:3)" In instances such as these, keeping silent is not loving. Speaking difficult truth — the truth of Christ and His Church — *that* is true love.

> "Speaking the truth in love, we are to grow up in every way into Him who is the head, into Christ, from whom the whole body, joined and knit together by every joint with which it is supplied, when each part is working properly, makes bodily growth and upbuilds itself in love (Ephesians 4:15-16)."

Now, that being said, some people (yes, even Christians) are far too quick and far too willing to point out all of their brothers' sins, and the sins of their brothers' brother, and his wife, and her aunt, and her cousin, and her co-worker, etc. Gossip is a sinful and deadly habit. Paul reminds us that we'd be wise to only offer fraternal correction after we've taken a long, hard look at ourselves. It's difficult to hold up a magnifying glass to someone else's life with a huge beam sticking out of our own eyes (Matthew 7:3-5).

The motivation of pointing out someone's sin is for his or her salvation and the good of the body, not for embarrassment and an increase in your reputation, appearance or station. True Christian brotherhood and sisterhood requires not only the willingness to point out (in love) someone else's sin, but the willingness to forgive the grievance, no matter how severe, even if it was inflicted upon you.

Fraternal correction is a common theme throughout St. Paul's writings. A closer examination of his work reveals a heart that understands the power of forgiveness, on personal and corporate levels (Romans 4:7-8). The more you pray and journal through Paul's writings, the more you'll see *what he saw*, namely that forgiveness requires power and not weakness (Galatians 6:1-10, Colossians 3:12-13, 2 Corinthians 7:8-9), and that power changes the world in a way that swords never could. Remember, we're still supposed to be "building one another up (Romans 14:19)."

It's been written that "To err is human, to forgive, divine." We know that sinning is human, but we sometimes forget that if we really want to be like Christ and live in His divine image, we must forgive. It is in forgiving that we are most like God.

And how do we forgive when we have been hurt? The answer is this: with love.

Do You Want the Good News or the Bad News?

The bad news is that if you follow Christ, you are going to die.

The good news is that Christ beat death, so follow Him and you will live.

The bad news is that following Him means *a lot* of personal sacrifice.

The good news is that He gives you the Holy Spirit to help you.

Let's explore each of these four truths, briefly, and one at a time.

The Bad News is that if You Follow Christ, You are Going to Die.

The Acts of the Apostles is one of the underrated jewels of the New Testament. Often called "the Gospel of the Holy Spirit," Acts bears witness to the explosion of the early Church through the power of the Spirit; it offers valuable insights into the early Saints, in particular, Peter and Paul.

The Acts of the Apostles was written by St. Luke, who was also a traveling companion of St. Paul. There is a line in the first chapter of Acts that is often glossed over by the "quick read," but (as is the case with most Scripture) a deeper, more prayerful reading of the verse opens up whole new levels of its meaning. We'll pause and pray through it, now, before we move on:

> "You shall receive power when the Holy Spirit has come upon you; and you shall be my witnesses...(Acts 1:8)"

Now, read the verse again, but instead of saying "witnesses," use the Greek word for "witness," which is *martyr*.

What does it take for someone to lay down their life for the Gospel? What does it take to turn Simon Peter, a fisherman, into *the* Shepherd? What does it take to turn Saul, a murderer, into a martyr? It takes a personal encounter with the living God, an intimate relationship with Jesus Christ.

If you have a difficult time really "connecting" with the saints and martyrs, it might be because they don't seem real to you. Possibly their sacrifice seems too great or their lives too noble, that it makes them almost "unreachable." Perhaps the stories read more like fiction then real life. Possibly, the faith has never come to life *in your life* in such a way that you'd offer your life. If that's the case, you're not alone. The pews are filled each week with people who have the desire to love God but who might fear total surrender to Him, to the point of death.

There is one very real "dilemma" every Christian must come to terms with, however, namely, that Jesus Christ is real and so are these disciples mentioned in Scripture. These are not fairy tales or legends. Paul walked the earth. Paul was stoned by others. Paul was whipped and flogged. Paul was shipwrecked and beaten and imprisoned (2 Corinthians 11:23-29) and beheaded, ultimately. These are real stories with real people and real life and death consequences.

This is so great a reality that the Church sets aside a feast day (June 28) just to commemorate the martyrdom of Sts. Peter and Paul. Pope Benedict XVI declared an entire "year of St. Paul" to commemorate the life and contribution of this heroic saint. Sts. Peter and Paul aren't remembered solely for their early church importance or accomplishments, but for their faithful martyrdom.

Do you see the importance of that proclamation of faith? Do you get it? People don't give their lives for ideas. People don't give their lives for philosophies. People don't even give their lives, necessarily, for wonder workers. People give their lives for truth and for freedom…they give their lives for the love of God.

If we spend more time focusing on what it takes to lay down our lives for *someone* (and not just *something*), we will begin to understand the difference between martyrdom and "senseless, historical homicide." Soon, we will see the intimacy with Christ required for such an act. Most of you reading this will never be asked to lay down your physical life for the Gospel. You will, however, be challenged several times a day or a week to lay down your life, in social situations, in tempting situations, in morally challenging situations; you will be asked to die to yourself and to public opinion, and to live for the truth of the Gospel.

How do you find the love and courage to die for the truth, for the faith, for *the* God?

The answer is this: with love.

Now, for the good news…

The Good News is that Christ Beat Death, so Follow Him and You Will Live.

Why do you go to Church? Why do you pray? Why do you listen to Christian music or wear a Christian t-shirt? Why do you serve at your parish or raise your family in the faith? Why do you go on retreats or head to Reconciliation when others don't?

You might have several different answers to the questions above, but they should all come from the same reason. St. Peter summed it up pretty well when he said, "…the goal of our faith is salvation (1 Peter 1:9)."

Do you get it? *Salvation* is the reason we "do the things we do" in our faith. Salvation, yours and others', is the reason you go to Mass. Salvation is why you and I should be willing to be witnesses (martyrs) with Christ for God's truth. We, like the apostles are commissioned to bring the Gospel to the ends of the earth (Matthew 28:16-20); commissioned means we are "co-workers" (1 Corinthians 3:9) in Christ's mission, offering truth to a world who desperately needs it, offering light to the blind and freedom to souls enslaved in darkness.

Perhaps you have people in your life, family members or friends, whom you desperately want to know the love of God. Have you ever wanted it for them more than they wanted it for themselves? Are there people in your life who look at Jesus as merely "a nice guy, with good stuff to say"?

Jesus is often seen as a philosopher more than as a Savior; "religion" has become a dirty word for a lot of people. It's unfortunate that in today's world, when so many people are in need of hope, looking for answers, and seeking clarity in their lives, that they overlook the one voice that is actually offering freedom and truth: the voice of Christ.

The question you might often hear from someone who is good-hearted but "anti-religion" is, "What difference does it make, really?" The answer is: all the difference in this *and* the next world.

The truth is that…

Without God, suffering is pointless.

Without God, our vocations (and our joy) become self-motivated.

Without God, other things like sex, work, money or relationships become our focus.

Without God, marriage is just a legal agreement.

Without God, there is no Heaven, when it's over, it's over; death is final.

But *with Christ*, everything changes.
As St. Paul pointed out:

With Christ, suffering has purpose (Romans 5:3, Ephesians 3:13, 2 Thessalonians 1:5, 2 Timothy 1:8; 2:3-9).

With Christ, our vocations bring freedom (Romans 8:28, 11:29; Ephesians 1:11, 2:10; Philippians 2:13, 1 Corinthians 1:26).

With Christ, we aren't mastered by the world (Romans 8:5-13, 13:14; Ephesians 5:3, Colossians 3:5, 1 Timothy 3:3, 2 Timothy 3:2, 1 Corinthians 5:11).

With Christ, marriage is a covenant of service (Romans 7:2-3, 1 Corinthians 7:2-4, Ephesians 5:23, 33; 2 Corinthians 11:2).

With Christ, death is defeated, life is eternal (Romans 2:7, 6:10, 22-23, 8:38; 1 Corinthians 15:47-48, 2 Corinthians 4:10-12, Ephesians 1:10, 3:15; Philippians 3:20, Colossians 1:5, 20; 1 Thessalonians 4:16, 5:8).

St. Paul understood that, in Christ, all things come into their proper perspective; jobs are just that, jobs. Money is something *not* everything. Marriage is a living example of love, not a dying example of annoyance. Through Christ, the big things don't overtake us and the little things have significance, again. With Jesus, you are never alone even when you feel lonely and never without hope even when you're feeling empty; God's love remains (1 Corinthians 13:13). That's the *good* news.

Jesus Christ offers us life. He also offers us a greater understanding and vision. With Jesus in your life, you begin to trust that there is a purpose you were created for and a vocation only you can fulfill (Jeremiah 29:11). God wants to reach those people in your life whom you're worried about and people whom you don't even know about (yet). The way He does that is the Gospel, and the way He delivers His Gospel is through you.

How do you do this, you may ask? How do you share the good news? With love.

The Bad News is that Following Him Means a lot of Personal Sacrifice.
Now, is this view of God we've spoken about thus far, St. Paul's "take" on the world, is this what you experience at school or at work? Is this the message modeled around the family dinner table? How about on MySpace? Is this the

message that you receive or that you spread on MySpace? If not, why not?

Remember, it was what Christ did with His body that demonstrated *Whose* He was. Are you willing to rise to St. Paul's challenge to "offer your body as a living sacrifice (Romans 12:1)"? Will you "refuse to conform yourself to this age (Romans 12:2)"?

Does your online profile on MySpace, for instance, need to change to better reflect the light of Christ? If so, change it. Does your demeanor at school or work need to change in order for people to know you take your faith seriously? If so, start changing. Does your dress, your attitude, your language, your gossip, your integrity, your modesty, your personality or anything else about yourself need an overhaul for people to really see Christ in you? St. Paul, like a good coach, would tell you to stand up and get at it, now, because there are souls at stake, including your own.

> "...cast off the works of darkness and put on the armor of light; let us conduct ourselves becomingly as in the day, not in reveling and drunkenness, not in debauchery and licentiousness, not in quarreling and jealousy (Romans 13:12-14)."

Oh, and he wasn't just picking on the Christians in Rome, either. No, St. Paul knew this would be a struggle for every Christian, us included. He makes similar points to the people in Ephesus (Ephesians 6:11-17), Thessalonica (1 Thessalonians 5:8) and Galatia (Galatians 1:4).

You might be asking yourself, "Why should I sacrifice like this, why should I change?" Well, it's because change is what it *really means* to be a true Christian. Christianity (as we see on the cross) means dying to yourself and to your own comforts so that others might live. It is difficult to do. It won't be easy. It won't be popular, most of the time. It never has been.

This is why St. Paul's words to the Romans are so timeless. The early Christians were going through the same struggles that we still do. He encouraged them to "put on the Lord Jesus Christ (Romans 13:14)," to clothe themselves in purity (like at your Baptism, see Galatians 3:27). Paul warned them never to become "a stumbling block or hindrance in the way of a brother (Romans 14:13)." And, he reminded us that, "each one of us shall give account of himself to God (Romans 14:12)." We will be held accountable and judged by how we sacrificed for others.

It's not enough to "talk about" Jesus with people. We need to do what the Incarnation did, we need to seek to *become* what God desires. We need to do what Jesus did on the cross, and "offer our bodies as a living sacrifice (Romans 12:1)."

Living like a Christian means that "if your brother is being injured by what you (do), you are no longer walking in love (Romans 14:15)." It means that we should look for ways to build one another up, not tear one another down (Romans 14:19). It means that it's not enough to look out for yourself only for your own holiness, but remember that "You who are strong ought to bear with the failing of the weak (Romans 15:1)." As "Christ became a servant (Romans 15:8)," we must become servants.

How can this become more than a nice idea?

The answer is this: with love.

How can you make MySpace more like *HisSpace?* That's right! With love.

The Good News is that He Gives You the Holy Spirit to Help You.
Most Catholics don't feel that they are worthy of sainthood. Let's face it, most of you reading this don't really believe that you could become or be considered a saint. "That's for people like Mother Teresa or Pope John Paul II," you'd probably say. "I'm not *that* holy," most would humbly offer. The truth of the matter, however, is that you are called to be a saint. The even greater truth (and better news) is that with the Holy Spirit, sainthood is actually attainable.

Do you want practical examples of how you become a saint? Let's look at what St. Paul says in Romans 12:9-21, but rather than reading it like a Scripture passage, we'll read it like a "laundry list." Here are the "twenty-five things you should do, daily, to become a living saint". It's actually pretty simple:

- Let (your) love be genuine
- Hate what is evil, hold fast to what is good
- Love one another with brotherly affection
- Outdo one another in showing honor
- Never flag (grow weary) in zeal
- Be aglow (on fire) with the Spirit
- Serve the Lord
- Rejoice in your hope
- Be patient in tribulation (suffering)
- Be constant in prayer
- Contribute to the needs of the saints
- Practice hospitality
- Bless those who persecute you, do not curse them
- Rejoice with those who rejoice
- Weep with those who weep
- Live in harmony with one another
- Do not be haughty

- Associate with the lowly
- Never be conceited
- Repay no one evil for evil
- Take thought for what is noble in the sight of all
- Live peaceably with all (as best you can)
- Never avenge yourselves, leave it to God
- If your enemy is hungry, feed him; if he is thirsty, give him drink
- Do not be overcome by evil, but overcome evil with good

Notice that, although I said sainthood is *simple* with this list, I didn't say *living* this was easy. Notice, too, that all of these commands are practical and active, just like all of St. Paul's advice. While Paul is very philosophical, he's also very practical. He doesn't want us to think that Christianity is all about "ideas" or "emotions (1 John 3:18)." These commands are rooted in the Gospels and remind us that our attitudes, decisions *and* our sins affect the entire body of Christ. We cannot be indifferent to one another or act blind to our own sins, because we are all one body, united in Christ (Romans 12:4-5).

Mark this page of the book. Let this list serve as the foundation for your daily life. Soon, you'll see why St. Paul refers to *this* (the word of God) as the "Sword of the Spirit" (Ephesians 6:17) and not a sword made of metal, the likes of which took his head and sent him home to heaven.

If this list struck you as "very difficult to do on a daily basis," that's good — it shows you're honest with yourself about where you are spiritually; that is self-awareness. This is hard to do. This is how you "offer your body as a living sacrifice (Romans 12:1)." This is what it means to live and love like Christ. The sacrifice of *one glorious body* upon a cross shows every *body* how to live and act as one body, in love...that we might live "no longer for ourselves, but for God (2 Corinthians 5:15)." That is how *MySpace* becomes *HisSpace,* how "virtual community" becomes true community and how our lives point one another back to God.

So, how do you do it? How can this become more than a nice idea, but the way you live your life daily? The answer, once again, is this: with love.

CHAPTER SIX

ON EARTH AS IT IS IN HEAVEN:
THE CHRISTIAN LIFE FROM HERE TO ETERNITY

I love music of all kinds. Everything from Baroque and Classical to Pop and Country has a place in my playlist. I think Mozart was a genius of the first order. I never get tired of tracks from groups like Third Day and U2. And Rascal Flatts' new album is in my iPod at this very moment.

Music is a gift from God. It is one of the most precious blessings we have received from the Almighty.

I am always amazed by how beautifully diverse music can be. And although my musical tastes tend to be pretty broad, there is one particular song that I'm not a big fan of. It is called "Big House," and I vividly remember the lyrics even though I haven't heard the song in over ten years. The music is fine. The tune is catchy. The beat is fun. There is nothing explicit or offensive in the song itself (in fact, the song is performed by a Christian band). No, my problem with the song stems from its description of eternity.

The song attempts to offer some thoughts and ideas about what things will be like after we die and go to heaven. It describes heaven as consisting of a "big yard" where the heavenly community can play football, a large table with an abundance of scrumptious food, and a big house with a surplus of nice, large rooms. Now, I appreciate what the song is trying to do. It's attempting communicate the desirability of heaven and how wonderful the next life will be for all those who die in Christ. This is true and good. The next life will indeed be wonderful. Heaven will consist of delight beyond our wildest imagination. The song is right to a point: heaven will be great. However, this is also where the song falls short. It doesn't make heaven *great enough*.

We are programmed by God for something bigger than ourselves. We have been searching for happiness ever since we were little kids. Every decision we make, whether it be to buy a toy, ride a bike, go to school, get married, or start a business is an attempt to find lasting happiness. Tragically, what so many people don't realize is that only in God will we ever find the lasting happiness we all crave.

If and when we make it to heaven, things like money, sex, football, and steak sandwiches (no matter how appealing now) will be the last things on our mind. Heaven is grounded in the life of God. God is the center of heaven. In Him — and in Him alone — will we find the happiness we spent our lives searching for. When we see and experience God as He is, money, sex, sports, and food will almost be repulsive compared to the pleasure we will experience in God.

Our finite minds cannot even begin to imagine how wonderful heaven really is. St. Paul himself emphasizes this fact when he remind us that "no eye has seen, nor ear heard, nor the heart of man conceived, what God has prepared for those who love him (1 Corinthians 2:9; Isaiah 64:4)."

The Next Life

Several years ago I read a book by a famous man who was attempting to persuade his readers that this life is all there is — that there is no life after death. The only thing that mattered, he argued, was the here and now. Everyone is given a set number of years to live and after that *nothing*. Game over. No more. Thus, the author's point was simple: live for today because today may be all you get. Spend your every waking moment in search of the greatest thrills and earthly pleasures you can find because this is all there is.

I remember being very depressed after reading that book. *Man*, I thought to myself, *if this is all that there is than everything is meaningless.* The television, Internet, and radio are filled with accounts of evil and injustice and pain and suffering. If this life is all that there is, then life is not a good thing…it's a curse.

Thanks be to God that this life isn't all that there is. There is life after death, and not just *any* life — the *greatest* life: the life of God Himself. St. Paul was deeply committed to the reality of life after death. Everything he did — every breath, every step, every word — was motivated and inspired by his belief in the reality of heaven. He dreamt of heaven. He longed to be with his Savior, with the King himself, Jesus. The motto, the vision, the inspiration of his life was the fact that for him "to live is Christ, and to die is gain (Philippians 1:21)."

Life wasn't easy for St. Paul. He was torn between two worlds. He was torn between this world, this life, and the people who still hadn't met Jesus, and the next world, where he could be with his Father and the glories of Heaven. The Apostle spoke about this tension on several occasions. He shared how he was "hard pressed between the two" and pulled in both directions. In all honesty,

Paul shared that his "desire [was] to depart and be with Christ, for that is far better" than this finite world in which we live (Philippians 1:23).

> "For to me to live is Christ, and to die is gain. If it is to be life in the flesh, that means fruitful labor for me. Yet which I shall choose I cannot tell. I am hard pressed between the two. My desire is to depart and be with Christ, for that is far better. But to remain in the flesh is more necessary on your account. Convinced of this, I know that I shall remain and continue with you all, for your progress and joy in the faith, so that in me you may have ample cause to glory in Christ Jesus (Philippians 1:21-26)."

This is one of the most moving passages we encounter in the writings of St. Paul. More than anything else, he desired final union with Jesus. He wanted to depart from this life so that he could pass into eternity and be with Christ, because "that is far better." I am almost moved to tears every time I read that verse for several reasons.

First, what incredible love St. Paul must have had for his Savior! Everyone wants to be loved. And one of the most difficult things for those deeply in love is to be separated from each other. One of my friends — who is now happily married to the man of her dreams — recounts a time in their engagement when she and her then-fiancé had to live in different states for a few months. They did their best to keep in touch via telephone, letters, and occasional visits (these were the days long before Internet and e-mail), but she shared how she was overcome with longing for her fiancé. This woman is not very dramatic — certainly not overly emotional — but she said that it was the first time in her life that she missed someone so much that it literally made her sick. The distance between them was so painful that she became physically ill.

This shouldn't surprise us. Love doesn't express itself in great distance and personal indifference. Quite the contrary: true love pulls at the deepest parts of our life and being and compels us to be united with the one we love. Love drives us to be with our beloved. Nothing is more difficult than separation from the person you love.

This is how St. Paul felt in his relationship with God. Now, obviously, he did not have any romantic feelings or sentiments for God in the same way that my friend had for her fiancé, but the apostle certainly felt a longing — an *aching* — for the one he loved more than life itself. Nothing was harder for St. Paul than being separated from his Lord. He endured many stonings, submitted to numerous whippings, and suffered from all forms of slander, starvation, and persecution for the sake of his beloved Jesus. And in the end all that he could think about was how much he yearned to be with Christ. The deepest longing of his heart was to be with Jesus. "My desire is to depart and be with Christ, for that is far better."

What amazing love! Although they churn out love story after love story, the greatest writers in Hollywood can't even begin to fathom a love like this! This is the kind of love that "does not insist on its own way…is not irritable or resentful…[but rather] bears all things, believes all things, hopes all things, endures all things (1 Corinthians 13:4-7)." St. Paul's every action was done out of his profound love for Jesus. And he held on to the hope that even though he couldn't see God face-to-face here on earth — "for now we see in a mirror dimly"— he would, one day, be able to bask in the glory and presence of his Lord and Savior and see him "face to face (1 Corinthians 13:12)."

"My desire is to depart and be with Christ, for that is far better…" The second reason why I am almost brought to tears when I read this selection from Paul's writing is this: *I often find my heart desiring things other than Christ…*In other words, *I'm not like St. Paul on this point; sadly, there are a lot of other things that I often put ahead of Jesus and desire over him.*

How many of us would answer "to be with Jesus in Heaven," if we were randomly asked, "What do you want more than anything else?" Sadly, almost none of us. We are so caught up in the flashy lights and cool sounds of this fallen world that very few of us ever look up to heaven with wonder and longing. We all want things. We all have desires. That's part of what makes us human. The problem isn't that we have desires; the problem is that we desire all the wrong things.

We Should Want More

A priest friend of mine was visiting a second grade class at a Catholic elementary school. He decided to begin his visit by asking the children what they wanted to be when they grew up. "Does anyone want to be a priest or a nun?" he asked. The kids stared at him in silence. No answer was given. "Okay, does anyone want to be a nurse or a doctor?" Again, blank stares. The priest was thrown by their lack of response so he asked them "well, then you tell me what do you want to be when you grow up?" Without missing a beat the entire class responded in unison: "I want to be rich!"

Sometimes it takes little children to speak the plain truth. We prefer the finite, small, temporal, passing, and (often) corrupt things of this world over the infinite splendor, joy and eternal treasure available in heaven. No one goes to bed at night dreaming and hoping for the joys of heaven. Rather, we go to bed hoping we will be able to have sex the following weekend, or that we will get invited to that party we heard our friends talking about, or that the cute guy from homeroom will notice us and ask us to prom. These are the kinds of things that occupy our minds, take up our time, and rule our lives. This is so sad. Not because money, sex, and power are intrinsically evil — they're not evil; God made them, and they are good when used in their proper context — no, it is sad because we don't see how *infinitely more satisfying the presence of God is over the best sex and the most money this world has to offer.* That's what is tragic.

Our problem is not that we desire too much. Our problem is that we desire too *little*. Again, St. Paul reminds us that "no eye has seen, nor ear heard, nor the heart of man conceived, what God has prepared for those who love him (1 Corinthians 2:9)." We have no "earthly idea" just how unspeakably delightful heaven will be. God wishes to give us more than we could ever imagine. He wants to fill us with the greatest happiness, the fullest pleasure, and the most abundant joy. The Psalmist says that in "[God's] presence there is fullness of joy, and in [his] right hand are pleasures for evermore (Psalms 16:11)."

What an incredible statement! In God there is fullness of joy and pleasures for evermore. This is so counter-intuitive. We tend to think of God and religion as impeding or preventing us from having joy and enjoying pleasure; but the Bible tells us that *the exact opposite is the case*. Only in God will our hearts find the joy and happiness they so desperately seek.

This is what St. Paul understood and what we habitually fail to recognize. We would much rather gorge ourselves with the rancid, dumpster scraps the world throws at us than dine at the most elegant and satisfying feast Jesus has set before us. We are all looking for love, happiness, joy, pleasure…and go looking for it in all the wrong places. Jesus is extending true love, true joy and true pleasure to us. It's almost like he's saying, "Look, here you go! I have what you're looking for. I have what your soul is craving! Follow me, I will show you where you can find a joy, happiness, and pleasure that will last for all eternity!"

And what do we do? We turn up our nose at his offer, shrug our shoulders in indifference, and walk away from what we need the most. What drives me to tears is that so many of us would rather have deformed, second-rate, fleeting pleasures like illicit sex, drugs and money than the infinite, the eternal, the everlasting and unchanging joy that God extends to us. How foolish can we be! God wants us to be happy — He wants us to be happy more than *we* want to be happy. He knows what will make us satisfied. He wants to lead us to the path of true happiness. But we turn Him down; we walk away, and prefer to feast out of the rancid dumpster of this fallen world than from the immaculate table of our Father's Heavenly Banquet.

A Desperate Plea…

I plead with you, if at this very moment you don't feel a deep longing to be with Christ, if the false and fleeting pleasures of this world are still more attractive to you than the infinite and lasting joys of Heaven itself, put down the book, get on your knees, and ask God to help you see what is truly beautiful, what is truly desirable, what is truly satisfying. Pray, asking for eyes to see and a heart to love. And if you don't know what (or how) to pray, say something like this:

Jesus, I know that only you are powerful enough to make me happy. I know that in you is found the "fullness of joy" and "pleasures forevermore." But, sometimes, I don't desire you above all. Sometimes I get confused and buy into the lie that the fleeting "pleasures" of this world will give me more happiness than you.

Help me to see through this lie. Help me to remember that only in you will I find the happiness I seek. I'm not interested in a happiness that lasts a few seconds, a pleasure that lasts a few days, a joy that lasts a few years — or even a few hundred years!

No, Jesus, I want a joy and a happiness and a pleasure that will last ten billion years and that is only the very beginning. Jesus, I want you. Only you will give the happiness that never ends. Only you can satisfy the deepest longings of my heart. Only you can fill me with the joy that I so desperately seek. So here I am — poor and weak, broken and bruised — but desirous of the peace which never ends…the joy that is only found in and through you.

Fill me with your presence. Give me this happiness. I love you. Amen.

Nothing can compare with the joy of knowing and being united with Christ. Nothing else, no matter how great, lasting, significant, or powerful it may seem here and now, can even begin to compare to the happiness that will come when we are united to Jesus in heaven. Everything else wanes in comparison to him.

This is why St. Paul could say that "my desire is to depart and be with Christ, for that is far better (Philippians 1:23)." Indeed it is far better…union with Jesus is better than anything we could ever imagine.

Our problem is not that we seek too great a joy or too immense a pleasure; but that we seek too little a joy and too small a pleasure.

Our Final Destination

The happiness and glory of heaven is the ultimate goal of all of reality. It is the treasure we are seeking. It is victory for which we are fighting. And, as St. Paul notes, it is the race we are running. "Do you not know that in a race all the runners compete, but only one receives the prize? So run that you may obtain it. Every athlete exercises self-control in all things. They do it to receive a perishable wreath, but we an imperishable. Well, I do not run aimlessly, I do not box as one beating the air; but I pommel my body and subdue it, lest after preaching to others I myself should be disqualified (1 Corinthians 9:24-27)."

It's amazing how hard people will work for something that is valuable. Men and women will devote their entire lives to accomplishing a handful of things. This is good. Things of great value are worth striving for. However, as great as earthly things may be; they will all pass away. No matter how sturdy your car, up-to-date your computer or fit your body is right now, they will all eventually fail and be replaced by something else.

St. Paul eagerly desired that we not devote ourselves to the pursuit of temporal, passing goods. He wants us to commit our lives to pursuing the *eternal Good*. Jesus. We are in a race. We are running for the goal. We are fighting for the prize. However, unlike "wreathes" or trophies which lose value, our reward isn't an object or a possession — it's a person: Jesus. This is what we're fighting for; this is what we're pursuing. This is whom we seek.

The race can be challenging. As we've already noted in earlier chapters, this life is not easy. There are many times when we'd like to give up, throw in the towel, and call it quits. But St. Paul urges us to press on even through the most arduous trials. The reward is worth it. The difficulties are real, but the everlasting sweetness of victory will make all of the pains and struggles seem like nothing in comparison. The Christian life is hard — *really hard*, at times. But we press on "because of the hope laid up for you in heaven (Colossians 1:3-5)."

When the body begins to ache and our desires begin to wander away from Heaven, we need to remain fixed on Jesus. This is not easy. St. Paul understood how challenging this race can be. He reminded us that "while we are at home in the body we are away from the Lord, for we walk by faith, not by sight." And although "we would rather be away from the body and at home with the Lord (2 Corinthians 5:6-8)," we remain vigilant because "our commonwealth [citizenship] is in heaven" and we "await a Savior, the Lord Jesus Christ (Philippians 3:20)."

This world is not our home. We are mere sojourners — we're just passing through. Our home is with Christ. We are citizens of heaven. Our unification in heaven was the plan from the very beginning. The Apostle tells us that "[God] made known to us in all wisdom and insight the mystery of his will, according to his purpose which he set forth in Christ as a plan for the fullness of time, to unite all things to him in heaven and things on earth (Ephesians 1:9-10)." This was God's original plan. He didn't design the world to be a "cosmic ant farm" that he could watch and enjoy. He created us so that we could be united to him and experience his eternal happiness, joy, and pleasure. This is his desire. This is his plan.

The *Catechism of the Catholic Church* states that this unity with God is the very definition of heaven. "This perfect life with the Most Holy Trinity — this communion of life and love with the Trinity, with the Virgin Mary, the angels and all the blessed — is called 'heaven.' Heaven is the ultimate end and fulfillment of the deepest human longings, the state of supreme, definitive happiness (CCC, 1024)."

Again, Heaven does not consist of sports, large rooms, and tasty food. Heaven consists of union with God. Heaven is being with and in God for all eternity. Period. And while that may sound boring and simple to us here and now, it's simply because we don't understand just who Jesus is. For if we truly understood how wonderful being with God in heaven really is, we would desire nothing else...ever. Heaven is gazing upon the infinite splendor and glory of God for all eternity.

Although it's impossible for us to imagine what that's like, one day we will see God as he is. And we will be so enraptured by his radiance that nothing else will be the center of our attention. This vision of God — seeing Him face to face — that St. Paul alludes to in 1 Corinthians 13:12 is known as the *beatific vision*. It is the essence of Heaven. It is the source of our everlasting happiness.

Vocation of Love

Each year, thousands of young people graduate from high school and college. Finally, after hundreds of hours of study, research, and classes, school is finally over. And while many of us experience great relief when we graduate, some of us are still haunted by this terrifying question: "What am I going to do with my life? I have a diploma. I've earned the degree. Now what?"

This is a very important question. It is a question of vocation.

"Vocation" isn't a common word in our modern time. It is rarely used and it is often misunderstood. Usually, when we hear the word "vocation," we tend to think of people called to the priesthood or religious life. This is true, priests and religious certainly do have a vocation, but this is only part of the picture. What is often forgotten is this essential fact: *everyone has a vocation*. No exceptions. While this may surprise you, it is absolutely true. Not everyone has a vocation to the priesthood or religious life, but everyone has a vocation to *love*.

The meaning of "vocation" is really quite simple: it is a divine "calling." A vocation is what one is called by God to do with his or her life. It is where we find meaning and fulfillment. A vocation gives us purpose. The *Catechism of the Catholic Church* states that the fundamental "vocation of humanity is to show forth the image of God and to be transformed into the image of the Father's only Son (CCC, 1877)."

Before anything else, we are called to be God's divinely adopted sons and daughters. God loves us so much that He not only forgives our sins but He also incorporates us into His divine family. We are His children (1 John 3:1). This was His plan and desire from the very beginning. St. Paul states that "before the foundation of the world," God chose us and "destined us in love to be his sons (Ephesians 1:4-5)." God loved us so much that He called us to be God's children. And it is only by fully embracing our Heavenly Father that we will find true, lasting happiness.

Again, sex won't give lasting happiness. Money can't purchase the joy we seek. Fame and power don't satisfy the deepest longings of our hearts. *These things — as good as they may be in their proper context — aren't powerful enough to give true happiness.* Only God is powerful enough make us eternally happy. Only he can satisfy our deepest longings.

Being a beloved child of God is the only thing that can give meaning to our lives. Life is difficult, and each individual vocation presents unique challenges and struggles. But we need not fear: we have a Father in Heaven who has promised never to leave or forsake us in times of difficulty (Hebrews 13:5). *Love is the key to sonship.* God's love for us is what makes us His divinely adopted children. *Our love for Him* is what makes us willing to do whatever He asks.

Every vocation entails sacrifice. A husband has to sacrifice himself for his wife — he has to put his own individual interests and desires second to those of his spouse. A mother has to sacrifice herself for her children. She has to give up everything from her time and energy to her comfort and interests for the sake of her children. A priest sacrifices himself for the Church and his parish community. He gives up the great blessing of having a natural family in order to serve God's supernatural family.

This is what our Heavenly Fathers has called us to do. He has called us to be His children. He has called to love Him and those around us without holding anything back. We can't "out-give" God. The more we love — the more we *give* — the more we will receive. God is love (1 John 4:8). He is the source of all happiness. It is through loving others that we, ourselves, will be truly happy.

I meet a lot of young Catholics who think that the secret to happiness is meeting Mr. or Miss "Right," or becoming "Fr. So-and-So." Vocations to marriage and priesthood are indeed wonderful callings with incalculable joys and blessings. However, vocations only work if we approach them asking "What can I give?" before we ask "What can I get?" It is through giving that we receive. It is through dying to self that we truly find life. It is through serving others that we are strengthened. This is what Jesus taught us and what we are called to do. And it is only through this kind of love — lived here on earth and perfected then in heaven — that we will find the happiness which never ends.

We need to follow St. Paul in making love our "aim" (1 Corinthians 14:1).

Everything we do needs to be firmly "rooted and grounded in love (Ephesians 3:17)" so that we might be fully united to Jesus in Heaven. God is love. It is who He is. It is what He does (Ephesians 2:4). May we be imitators of him. May we love here on earth as our Heavenly Father loves eternally in Heaven.

It is important to remember that love doesn't begin in Heaven; it has to start in our hearts here on earth. But we can also take great comfort in the fact that love doesn't end after our time on this world is over; it is only just beginning.

Enduring Love

Things will be different in heaven. You won't get tired. Sleep will no longer be needed. Fun and games won't be as important to you. There will be no sadness. No crying. No weeping or mourning. Heaven is full of infinite joy and happiness. All of the things that concerned and worried us here on earth will no longer be a source of anxiety. The only thing that will be at the center of our Heavenly lives is *love*.

In one of his most famous chapters, St. Paul describes the nature of love and speaks of it like this:

> "Love never ends; as for prophecies, they will pass away; as for tongues, they will cease; as for knowledge, it will pass away. For our knowledge is imperfect and our prophecy is imperfect; but when the perfect comes, the imperfect will pass away...For now we see in a mirror dimly, but then face to face. Now I know in part; then I shall understand fully, even as I have been fully understood. So faith, hope, love abide, these three; but the greatest of these is love (1 Corinthians 13:8-13)."

Let's take a moment to look at this significant passage very carefully. The Apostle begins by noting that "love never ends." This is striking. There are a lot of things that will end when we get to heaven. Sin does not exist in heaven. When you're in the presence of God — enveloped in His glory and love — sinful thoughts and actions will be impossible. You will be so caught up in his beauty and splendor, no evil thought will enter your mind even for a split second.

Your earthly concerns and fears will vanish. Your difficulties and confusions will be resolved. When you see your Heavenly Father as He is in all of His glory, love is the only thing that will remain. Nothing else will matter. Nothing else will occupy your mind or grab your attention. God — and God alone — will be your joy and your delight.

"Love never ends." It is amazing that of all the things here on earth, love is only thing that will remain constant from this life into the next life. St. Paul notes that right now "our knowledge is imperfect…We see in a mirror dimly." God is so much greater than we are that our frail human minds can't perceive and understand his splendor. That is why we need faith. Faith is a gift from God that enables us to know things which surpass our natural abilities.

For example, I don't need faith to believe that two plus two equals four. Why? Because my mind can understand this simple equation. Simple arithmetic is not above my mind's capability. I can understand that two plus two equals four without supernatural assistance. However, the doctrine of the Trinity does require faith. Why? Because this is something that a human mind would never be able to figure out on its own. A human mind can solve a simple math problem, but a human mind cannot solve the mystery of God being Father, Son, and Holy Spirit; three in one.

That is why God had to reveal this truth to us. He knew that we would never figure it out on our own, so He had to reveal it through the Bible and the teaching of the Church. We believe that the Trinity is true not because we fully understand it, but because God told us it is true. This is the definition of supernatural faith — believing something we can't figure out on our own because God reveals it to us.

Faith exists here on the earth. I don't see God face-to-face here and now. I don't "see" Jesus in the Eucharist. My human eyes aren't powerful enough to discern his divine presence. Is he really there? Yes! Do I believe it? Absolutely! However, faith will not exist in Heaven. "Belief" will no longer be necessary when we're united with God in his heavenly Kingdom.

Why is this? Why does faith exist on earth and not in heaven? The answer is simple: when we're in heaven, we will be able to *see* God as he is. Right now, I can't see God directly. Therefore I have faith — I believe what God has said but I cannot see. When I'm in heaven, however, I won't have to "believe" it. I'll know it. When I'm in heaven I will be able to see him for myself; faith will no longer be necessary. As St. Paul says, "Now I know in part; then I shall understand fully (1 Corinthians 13:12)."

Hope is another thing that exists on earth but does not exist in heaven. When I "hope" for something, I desire something that I do not (yet) possess. When I say "I hope I get an 'A' on my math test," I mean that I have not yet received an 'A' on my test. We "hope" for things that we do not have. I do not "hope" for an 'A' on my test if I already have an 'A' on my test. We hope for things that we wish to obtain.

However, when we're in heaven, we will no longer have to "hope" for the glory of Christ because we will be in its presence. It will no longer be far off, in the future. When in heaven, we will possess the infinite joy and happiness we spent our whole lives "hoping" to attain — we will finally have it. Like faith, hope only exists on earth. When we get to heaven faith and hope will disappear because we will see God as He is and have the joy that is only found in Him.

Faith ends. Hope ends. But "love never ends." In fact, rather than disappearing once we enter into the glories of Heaven, love finds its ultimate perfection — it doesn't stop once we get to Heaven; it gets even better! Love is supreme because it is *permanent*. We won't be the least bit disappointed that heaven is not a "big house" full of room, food, and football games. We will be overcome with the everlasting pleasure and delight of being enveloped in God's love. For it is as St. Paul so beautiful states: "faith, hope, love abide, these three; but the greatest of these" — the one thing which will last from now into eternity — "is love (1 Corinthians 13:13)."

CONCLUSION

CHOOSE YOUR OWN ADVENTURE:
THE PRACTICALITY OF ST. PAUL

I mentioned in the introduction that my favorite book to look at was our Catholic picture Bible. My favorite books to *actually read* were from a series called *Choose Your Own Adventure*. Some of you reading this might remember them. Every page offered you a situation and two choices. One choice led you to one page, the other choice led you to a different page, and each page contained more choices and so on. Your story ("adventure") ended differently and at different times, depending upon what you chose on the page prior. It was a nice metaphor for life, even if I didn't know at the time what a "metaphor" was...I just liked the empowerment of making choices at such a young age. I liked the notion of controlling my destiny.

God gives you free will. Your life is in your hands. Additionally, allowing His life to work through you (or not) is your decision. Saul had an encounter with Christ and then he had a choice to make. He chose to serve God. Next came the choice of whether or not to change his approach to faith, and he said yes. Next came the calling to preach in Christ's name. Again, he said yes.

Paul's story (life) was, really, a "choose your own adventure" of sorts...he was faced with decision after decision — choose himself or choose Christ. Your life is no different. Today you will be given the choice of whether to live for God or for yourself (Deuteronomy 30:15-20). You'll probably be given several opportunities to choose between God and self today, actually. Let's say that the new adventure of your life starts right now.

So the question is this: how far are you willing to go for God?

How Far Are You Willing To Go?

Following this paragraph are ten questions. The questions are straightforward and seem simple enough. Saying "yes" to each is easy, but living "yes" on a daily basis is quite difficult.

St. Paul had to answer each of these questions, internally first, before living them "externally". His life became a living proclamation of his "yes" to each. If your response to each one is yes, continue reading. If your response to one (or several) of the questions is "no," however, stop reading and spend some time in prayer, asking the Holy Spirit to open your mind and heart to the areas that need to change in your life right now.

1. Are you willing to be uncomfortable for God?
2. Are you willing to trust God completely?
3. Are you willing to surrender "your plans" and "your life" to Him?
4. Are you willing to really "let God into" your sin?
5. Are you willing to change sinful environments and relationships in order to live a more holy life?
6. Are you willing to personally sacrifice so that others might know Christ?
7. Are you willing to try new things in your prayer life, home life, parish life, school and work life?
8. Are you willing to seek God more proactively and more urgently?
9. Are you willing to protect your state of grace more vigilantly?
10. Are you willing to share God's grace with *all* whom He puts before you?

Notice that these questions said "willing," not "able". The apostles weren't able to do anything heroic or miraculous by themselves, not without the power of Christ, not without the Holy Spirit. By ourselves we are nothing but with the Holy Spirit, St. Paul reminds us that "(we) can do all things (Philippians 4:13)."

St. Paul understood that he was nothing without God, but that with God he was powerful beyond measure. His whole life became an attempt to allow God's life to overtake and consume "his life." As we stated in the introduction, St. Paul wasn't writing or preaching "another Gospel." For Paul, it wasn't about recording or re-telling what Jesus said or did, it was about *living and becoming what Christ said to do,* daily and in practical ways.

In this final chapter, we're going to take a *very brief* look at each of these ten questions and discuss in **practical terms**, what each ones means to you and to your daily faith walk.

Remember, this adventure is yours. You get to choose if you "move on" to the next question or not. Your honest response should dictate if you continue reading or pause to pray.

To quote *Indiana Jones and the Last Crusade,* "Choose wisely."

1. Are you willing to be uncomfortable for God?

Remember the conversion of Saul that we mentioned a little earlier? Ever wonder what kept Paul going for so many miles and for so many years? Remember what all he went through?

> "Five times I have received at the hands of the Jews the forty lashes less one. Three times I have been beaten with rods; once I was stoned. Three times I have been shipwrecked; a night and a day I have been adrift at sea; on frequent journeys in danger from rivers, danger from robbers, danger from my own people, danger from Gentiles, danger in the city, danger in the wilderness, danger at sea, danger from false brethren; in toil and hardship, through many a sleepless night, in hunger and thirst, often without food, in cold and exposure, and, apart from other things, there is the daily pressure upon me of my anxiety for all the churches (2 Corinthians 11:24-28)."

So why did he keep at it? Why didn't he just "set up shop" in Damascus, writing letters and waiting for people to come to him to hear him preach? The simple answer would be that Jesus, Himself, "went out" to the sinners and outcasts. That, in turn, is what an apostle is: one who is "sent forth". Those answers are correct on both counts, but to say that they were the *only* reasons would be selling Paul short. No, for Paul it wasn't just occupational, it was personal.

Paul was used to living out his religious beliefs; he was a Pharisee. After experiencing the mercy of Christ firsthand, however, Paul's attitude changed. It wasn't just about the *what* of his religion, but about the *Who.*

You should have the same goal. Your Catholic faith ought to be about a relationship with a *Who* (God), not just participation in a *what* (the Church). When your faith is centered around God, around the *Who* and not just the *what,* everything changes. You'll go to Mass out of love not just obligation. You'll serve with joy, not out of guilt. You'll confess out of desire to grow in holiness, not just a desire to avoid hell.

When it's personal, you're willing to be uncomfortable because you're in relationship with God. When it's cold and impersonal, every sacrifice has the potential of creating bitterness or resentment within your soul. Base your faith on a personal, intimate relationship with Jesus Christ and watch how comfortable you'll get being uncomfortable.

If you can say yes to being uncomfortable for God, move on to the next question. If you are unwilling to be uncomfortable for God, pray about it more before moving on.

2. Are you willing to trust God completely?

Trust might be the one area that every Christian struggles with the most. We have an easy time telling others to trust God, but when it comes to us trusting Him we are reluctant to let go of control and let God be God. Trusting in God requires (and challenges) the theological virtues. Faith, hope and love are not merely "head things;" each virtue (properly lived out) necessitates action on our part. We demonstrate what we believe not in words but in actions. Actions follow beliefs.

Consider this famous story:

> "A huge crowd was watching the famous tightrope walker, Blondin, cross Niagara Falls one day in 1860. He crossed it numerous times — a 1,000 foot trip, 160 feet above the raging waters. He not only walked across it; he also pushed a wheelbarrow across it.
>
> One little boy just stared in amazement. So after completing a crossing the fellow looked at that little boy and he said, "Do you believe I could take a person across in the wheelbarrow without falling?"
>
> "Yes, sir. I really do," The fellow says. "Well then, get in, son."[10]

It's not enough to "say" you trust God or to tell others to trust Him. Are you willing to put your money where your mouth is and "get into His wheelbarrow?"

In order to grow in your faith, you must trust God, for He is the means and the end of your pursuit. If this is a struggle for you, you must at the very least be willing to admit to Him that you struggle in trusting Him; even admitting it is, in essence, a sign of your trust in His mercy.

Tell God that you don't understand everything He has planned for you but that you trust Him. Say to Jesus that you are scared but that you want to trust Him more completely. Invite Christ into your life, job, future, relationship, marriage or friendship, and surrender control. He didn't promise us it would be easy, but He did promise us that He is closer than we might think, more aware than we might give Him credit for, and more loving than we can possibly comprehend.

If you trust God, move on to the next question. If you don't truly trust God, pray about it more before moving on.

3. Are you willing to surrender "your plans" and "your life" to Him?

Now, you're willing to trust God. That is excellent. What does a trusting relationship look like? Saying "I trust you" is easy (or maybe not, depending how you responded to the previous question), but moving beyond the words and living out "I trust you, God" in action is challenging. How do you get to a point where God is in control of your life and it's not *you* in control of *your* life, simply asking God to agree with your plans?

That's where we go wrong most of the time: We look at our lives as our own. We forget who the Creator is in the equation. We ignore the Author of our stories. The Divine Author has a story written for you, however, and it's time you prayerfully opened up to it.

God is pro-life in the obvious sense (anti-murder/abortion) and in the less obvious sense…He has an expectation for us to bear fruit (Genesis 1:28, John 15:16).

God created you for good works (Ephesians 2:10). Likewise, God created you with a purpose that only *you* can fulfill (Jeremiah 1:4-8). You have a calling in life. You have a mission that he designed specifically for you (Psalm 139:14-16), as we talked about in the last chapter.

Often times we fear saying yes to God because we don't trust where He is going to take us. We're afraid that His plan is going to be boring, too hard or too constraining to what we want. St. Paul reminds us that with God we have nothing to fear (2 Timothy 1:7). His plan is better than ours (Jeremiah 29:11-12). God will take care of you. Put your trust in God. In the end you'll not only be faithful, you'll be more joyful. The point is, if you want to be happy and have a fulfilling life, take time now to get to know the Author of that life. He won't steer you wrong, ever.[11]

If you will surrender your plans in favor of God's plans, move on to the next question. If you won't let go of your plans, pray about it more before moving on.

4. Are you willing to really "let God into" your sin?

Do you play hide and seek with God? Adam did, and look where it got him.

Do you think you can hide your sins from God? Even if you have successfully hidden sins from everyone else in your life until now, God knows. He knows the worst thing you've ever done (the thing that maybe your friends and family don't even know) and he sees the best that you can be *through Him* (something that you might not even realize yourself). Christ is waiting to forgive you and to heal you, not waiting to condemn you. Don't pretend the sin isn't there. Don't fool yourself into thinking that if the rest of your life appears perfect to the world that God sees it the same way.

Are you *real* with Jesus? Do you invite Jesus into every corner of your life? Not just the polished rooms that you are proud to display? Do you invite Jesus into the darkest recesses of your soul? Do you let Jesus roll up His sleeves and get to work on those corners of your spiritual "house" that remain cluttered, dirty or just plain untouchable? Do you invite Him into your soul's "garage," show him into the "attic," or invite the Lord to root around in the "closets" of your soul, cluttered with sin, failure and shame?[12]

Jesus was born into a messy manger. Jesus died on a messy cross. He rose again to conquer your mess. Jesus isn't afraid of your mess. Don't be afraid of his grace, healing and forgiveness.

If you will be authentic and let God into your sin, move on to the next question. If you are too ashamed to let God in, pray about it more before moving on.

5. Are you willing to change sinful environments and relationships in order to live a more holy life?

Have you ever said to yourself (in regards to Confession), "I feel like such a failure…I just keep on sinning, and I just keep on confessing the *same sins"?* If so, you're not alone, the greatest saints had the same struggle. Eventually, though, virtue won out for them and it can win out for you.

Often times we deal with the effects of sin, but not the roots of it. It's like we are drowning in a river of water and the priest (Christ) keeps pulling us out (Confession). It's not until we are on dry ground, though, and we proactively walk *upstream* to find the source of the water (sin) that we can really do anything about it. For some people the river is drunkenness but the source is an addiction to alcohol. For others the sin is masturbation but the source is an addiction to pornography. The further "upstream" we walk, the deeper we find the roots of those addictions, like fear, loneliness, depression, anger, abandonment, low self-esteem, etc. It's often like your body and soul are immersed in a deadly and painful tug-of-war and you feel helpless in the battle. As we noted in earlier (see chapter four), St. Paul knew the conflict all too well:

> "I do not understand my own actions. For I do not do the thing that I want, but I do the very thing that I hate…so then it is no longer I that do it, but sin which dwells in me (Romans 7:15-17)."

It's not enough to recognize the sins we commit, we must prayerfully seek out their source(s). If we don't get to the root of our sin, our flesh and spirit will be in constant battle. True freedom means, first, locating the sources of our sin and, second, surrendering them to Christ. It is in that surrender, you will finally taste true freedom.

> "For those who live according to the flesh set their minds on the things of the flesh, but those who live according to the Spirit set their minds on the things of the Spirit. To set the mind on the flesh is death, but to set the mind on the Spirit is life and peace (Romans 8:5-6)."

Realize, too, that the minute you start asking questions like "Where does my sin come from?" or "How can I eliminate these sins, Lord?", you will be attacked. Paul reminds us a few verses later that "when (I) you want to do right, evil is at hand (Romans 7:21)." The devil doesn't want you to realize these sources of sin, as they are his greatest weapon against you and the means by which he keeps us enslaved to sin and suffocated in his grip.

If you are willing to let God remove and destroy sinful relationships and environments in your life, move on to the next question. If you won't surrender causes of sin to God your Father, pray about it more before moving on.

6. Are you willing to personally sacrifice so that others might know Christ?

Earlier in this chapter, we asked "How far are you willing to go?". What are you willing (and not willing) to do for God in order to better live out your faith?

Let's find out.

Would you get rid of your Internet?
Would you get rid of your television?
Would you get rid of your iPod?
Would you get rid of any CDs that didn't lead you closer to Him?
Would you get rid of your video games?
Would you break up with your boyfriend/girlfriend?
Would you stop abusing your sexuality?
Would you never look at pornography again?
Would you go to counseling with your husband/wife?
Would you forgive *all those* who have hurt you?
Would you seek forgiveness from all those you have hurt?
Would you stop drinking alcohol?
Would you never touch drugs again?
Would you invite your neighbors, classmates or co-workers to Church?
Would you reach out to the least popular and least "liked" people around you?
Would you offer friendship to those who most "annoy" you?

Would you change your college major?
Would you change or quit your job?
Would you check out a seminary or convent?
Would you give away most of your clothes?
Would you arrange your schedule to get to Adoration every day?
Would you move to another country to tell people about Jesus?
Would you donate your time to do service once a week?

Now, there are certain things on this list you shouldn't be doing anyway (like drugs, abusing sexuality, looking at pornography, etc.). The bigger question is whether anything on this list is difficult for you to say no to doing. Is there anything here that you just "can't do" or (more to the point) "won't do" for God? Are you willing to sacrifice, personally, until it hurts?

Remember these two verses we spoke about earlier?

> "I appeal to you therefore, brethren, by the mercies of God, to present your bodies as a living sacrifice, holy and acceptable to God, which is your spiritual worship. Do not be conformed to this world but be transformed by the renewal of your mind, that you may prove what is the will of God, what is good and acceptable and perfect (Romans 12:1-2)."

Commit them to memory. Pray them every time you pass by a crucifix. Pray them every time you see the body of Christ elevated at Mass. Pray them every time you feel tempted to be selfish. Pray them every time you are tempted sexually. Pray them every time someone makes you feel "foolish" for believing this "fairy tale" message of Christ in the 21st century.

If you are willing to sacrifice (even if it hurts), move on to the next question. If you don't want to sacrifice in your life, pray about it more before moving on.

7. Are you willing to try new things in your prayer life, home life, parish life, school and/or work life?

Rethinking Your Prayer Life
Why pray? Seriously, why do we pray? Is it to "get" things from God? Is it to change the way things are going in our lives? Is it to thank God, or worship Him? Is it to become more like Christ? Is it to understand God better or to "get Him" to understand you better? Be honest.

Practically speaking, prayer becomes more challenging the less we do it. The more we try, the more we practice, the more time we actually set aside to do it the more comfortable we'll become with it.

Prayer is the great gift of our existence; prayer is the ability to step out of ourselves and out of our circumstances, the ability to leave behind the frustrations and anxieties of the day and to just throw ourselves into the arms of God. Consider what these saintly souls had to say about prayer:

"Prayer is the best weapon we possess, the key that opens the heart of God."
— St. Padre Pio

"Change your hearts…unless we change our hearts we are not converted. Changing places is not the answer. The answer is to change our hearts. And how do we change? By praying."
— Blessed Mother Teresa

"How to pray? This is a simple matter. I would say: Pray any way you like, so long as you do pray."
— Blessed Pope John Paul II

"Often the mere babblings of a child will touch his father in heaven."
— St. John of the Ladder

"Lord, teach me to seek you, and reveal yourself to me as I look for you. For I cannot seek you unless you first teach me."
— St. Ambrose

"Prayer is the place of refuge for every worry, a foundation for cheerfulness, a source of constant happiness, a protection against sadness."
— St. John Chrysostom

"Souls without prayer are like bodies, palsied and lame, having hands and feet they cannot use."
— St. Teresa of Avila

"However softly we speak, he is near enough to hear us."
— St. Teresa of Avila

"Do not distress yourself about your prayers. It is not always necessary to employ words, even inwardly, it is enough to raise your heart and let it rest in our Lord…"
— St. Francis De Sales

"We must pray literally without ceasing – without ceasing; in every occurrence…a habit of lifting up the heart to God, as in a constant communication with Him."
— St. Elizabeth Seton

"You don't know how to pray? Put yourself in the presence of God, and as soon as you have said, "Lord, I don't know how to pray!" you can be sure you have already begun."
— St. Josemaría Escrivá

The Church offers us so many different forms of prayer, some free-form and some more focused. No matter how awake or tired your mind, no matter how alert or fatigued your heart, there is always a form of prayer available to lead you deeper into the tireless heart of God.

Adoration of the Blessed Sacrament, the Rosary, the Liturgy of the Hours, journaling, praise and worship, sacred silence, *lectio divina*, the Stations of the Cross and fasting are all forms of prayer that can transform the mundane life into encounters of God's grace. When all else fails, never doubt or forget the power of simply praying and calling upon the name of Jesus; that prayer alone, praying the name above all names (Philippians 2:10-14), is one of the greatest actions we could ever attempt.

Discover (or re-discover) different forms of prayer and break out of any spiritual "ruts" that may creep into your prayer life. Most importantly, commit yourself to daily prayer, praying the Scriptures and frequenting the Sacraments.

Rethinking Your Home Life
It is usually a lot harder to be a "good Christian" in our own homes or around our own friends than it is to be around strangers.

Why is that?

Usually it's because those we're closest to see us at our worst...all those times that we don't act "real Christian," those times that we are selfish, rude or impatient. Some people feel it is okay to scream at their spouses or children because families have to love you anyway. Others feel it is okay to scream at the world because "who cares" if they love you back.

In either case, we would be shortsighted to think that such conduct is admissible or encouraged by Christ. If you can't envision Joseph screaming at Mary or Mary yelling at Jesus, it's a good rule of thumb that it's not what Jesus would want you to do, either. Think about it.

You have been "purchased at a great price," as St. Paul reminds us (1 Corinthians 6:20). You have a responsibility to live the Gospel message, beginning with your own home. You have to find (and create) ways to share Christ's love, especially those in your home. Do this non-verbally even more than verbally. Come up with a list of "things" you can do to share love in your home. Especially try to think of things that stretch you, things that might "hurt" a little at first...things that will take a shot at your pride. Next, do them.

Your example of Christ (at home and abroad) should be like St. Paul's; your faith needs to be:

- Practical, so people can relate
- Relevant, to effect peoples' lives daily
- Simple, so people will remember
- Personal, to show you know Him
- Joyful, to be something that is attractive
- Real, to speak the truth with authenticity

Yes, some people are going to think you're nuts but, then again, some aren't. Don't worry about what people think. People think all kinds of things, but that doesn't mean that their thoughts are God's thoughts (Isaiah 55:8-9).

Rethinking Your Parish Life

One of the places we most clearly see our Christian solidarity (as we discussed in Chapter Five) is within the Holy Mass (Liturgy). When someone says, "I'm a Christian, I just don't believe in organized religion, why can't I just pray alone?", St. Paul's response would be, "You *can and should* pray alone, never cease praying (1 Thessalonians 5:17)", but true Christians understand that they are "members of one another" (Romans 12:4) and that "none of us lives to himself (Romans 14:7)". We should never neglect or reject the gathering together of God's people in worship (Hebrews 12:25). Everything I do affects the rest of the living body of Christ. Everything that you do affects the body, too, for better or for worse.

Since we are so intimately connected and since our souls and lives are so intertwined in this mystical body of Christ, it is only natural that we would (and should) worship *together* (see Matthew 18:20). Worship is the most intimate expression of our love for God, a humble and passionate response to His sovereignty. Read the *Acts of the Apostles;* the early Christians worshiped together. Their example is meaningful, essential and timeless; and this is why we are called never to worship singularly - as one - but communally, as one body.

How "connected" would we *truly* be to the body of Christ if we desired *only* to be separate and alone when we worship? The same perspective applies to other elements of living as one body. Do you tithe back to the parish? Do you participate in Church functions? Do you engage in the community or run for the parking lot following Mass? Are you serving within the parish community? Are you involved in a ministry?

If we are *truly one body* as St. Paul challenges us to be, these questions need to be asked and, if necessary, perspectives and practices need to change. Take a hard look at how you approach your time at the parish and ask yourself if there is something "more" you could be doing for the Kingdom.

Rethinking Your School Life or Work Life

Whether you are still in school or are member of the full-time work world, "rethinking" your school/work life can often be like "rethinking" your diet...you know you need to make some changes, but you really don't want to do it. Rather than get into all the things you might need to change about your own identity in these settings, let's focus on what God might be wanting from you in these places. There are souls He wants to touch through your example.

To be honest, God has probably already revealed to you the people in these settings who most need Christ *in you*. There are far too many examples of people in need to give here, but allow me to offer a few to consider:

At School
"That girl" in class who is the most quiet usually has some of the most meaningful things to say, but she is probably fearful to say them for a variety of reasons. Reach out to her.

"That guy" in class who is always sarcastic or cutting is usually the one who is the most insecure, and he tries to hide that fact in the process. Reach out to him.

At Work
"That guy" in the office who is the most outspoken and opinionated professionally, is usually the least confident, personally. Model humility.

"That woman" in the office who is the most forward or immodest on the exterior, is usually the most wounded on the interior. Affirm her interior.

These are just a few examples. They are not offered to dismiss the hurtful actions of others, merely to offer a different perspective on people whose lives and decisions might make your faith walk a little more challenging.

You're still called to be Christ to them...even when it's hard. We're called to be Christ even when the people we're trying to help ignore, reject, and ridicule us. Be prepared: this lifestyle of radical love is not easy, but it's infinitely worth it. If you truly commit yourself to being Christ to all people you will face many struggles and great opposition. But be not afraid. Both Jesus and St. Paul knows what it's like to be rejected by those you love, and this is why the Apostle tells us to stand firm in our commitment to the "high road" of love, "living a life worthy of the call you have received (Ephesians 4:1)."

In all of these cases, from your personal prayer life to your home life, from your parish life to your work and school life, the common denominator is change. Are you willing to do things differently? Are you willing to approach God differently? Are you willing to approach your family members with more love and understanding? Are you willing to lead more by your example of holiness?

If you are willing to radically change your prayer life, home life, parish life and school/work life, move on to the next question. If you are resistant to change, pray about it more before moving on.

8. Are you willing to seek God more proactively and more urgently?

As was mentioned earlier, the Sacraments are our most perfect, most physical encounter of Christ's grace that the Church has to offer. The Sacraments were instituted by Christ, Himself, and two of them, specifically, are especially important for us to be able to live out this Christian life that St. Paul points us toward: Eucharist and Reconciliation.

Rearrange your schedule to insure that you encounter Christ's grace in the Sacraments more regularly and more intentionally. Doing so would include:

- Going to Daily Mass
- Spending at least an hour a week in Adoration of the Blessed Sacrament
- Frequenting the Sacrament of Reconciliation (at least once a month)
- Praying the Sunday Readings in the days prior to Mass, to be prepared

Remember, it wasn't until St. Paul had encountered Christ personally and physically (as we do in the Sacraments) that he could fulfill his vocation. St. Paul didn't just encounter Christ once, but constantly, in the Eucharist.

St. Paul *vehemently defended* the Real Presence of Jesus in the Eucharist (1 Corinthians 11:23-29). And it's important to note that even though St. Paul wasn't present at the Last Supper, he fully received (and, in turn, handed on) the *living tradition* of the Eucharistic sacrifice, safeguarded by the Apostolic Tradition (2 Thessalonians 2:15). The "bread" is not mere bread. The "wine" is not mere wine. It is nothing less that Jesus himself… full and complete: *body, blood, soul and divinity.*

The Catholic Church has always taught that Christ did, indeed, die once and for all as "a single sacrifice for sins (Hebrews 10:11-12)." Thus the Church *does not teach that we are re-sacrificing Jesus Christ during Mass.* Christ's loving sacrifice on the Cross over two thousand years ago can never be repeated — it's impossible to repeat something that never ended. In addition, the effects of that loving sacrifice will never be exhausted. Thus, the Mass does not re-sacrifice

Jesus, but it does *represent* (re-present) His one sacrifice; enabling us to receive the fullness of His loving Presence.

The Mass is serious because Jesus is serious. St. Paul felt so strongly about the fact that the bread and wine are *truly* transubstantiated into Christ's flesh and blood, that he strictly warned followers who are in a state of serious (mortal) sin, "not to partake, lest they eat and drink judgment unto themselves (1 Corinthians 11:27-29)." We dare not receive Jesus' holy presence in the Eucharist unless his divine life (i.e., grace) is present in our souls.

Jesus commanded us to celebrate the Mass in "remembrance of me (Luke 22:19-20)." He commanded us to "become one (member) *with*" Him, through the Eucharist. We intimately become one with Christ, again and again, through the Sacraments; for that is what it truly means to be "re-membered" by God — to be filled with the fullness of His divine life and presence.

To state things clearly, it's not so much a matter of us consuming *Christ* as it is of Christ consuming *us* in the Eucharist…He is received into us and *we* are received *into* Him. What a glorious mystery this is! How incredible it is that we, mere humans, are blessed enough to partake own God's own divine nature (2 Peter 1:4). How loved we are to become one with God and have our lives joined to His.

St. Paul did not believe that the Eucharist is merely a *symbol*. He believed that it is "really" *Jesus*. This is why he took the Eucharist so seriously in his writings… and this is why *we* need to take his writings about the Eucharist very seriously in our lives. And he wasn't the only saint who proclaimed Christ's true presence in the Eucharistic sacrifice. St. Cyril of Jerusalem, St. Irenaeus, St. Justin Martyr, St. Augustine — all four of these famous early Church fathers (and countless more) have attested to the real presence of Christ in the Eucharist.

It may look like typical bread, it may taste like simple wine, but it is nothing less than the body and blood of our sovereign Lord, Jesus Christ. St. Paul reminded us that "as often as you eat this bread and drink the cup, you proclaim the Lord's death until he comes (1 Corinthians 11:26)."

If you will become more "Sacramental", move on to the next question. If you don't want to become more Sacrament-based, pray about it more before moving on.

9. Are you willing to protect your state of grace more vigilantly?

We're taught that we need to be in a "state of grace" prior to receiving the Eucharist. In other words, if we have committed a mortal sin, we ought not to receive Communion without first going to the Sacrament of Reconciliation. Thus, sin threatens and destroys our state of grace.

Now, how do you change your approach in such a way that you are not only trying to avoid sin but to *preserve your state of grace?* How do you stay rooted in Christ and "protect" your state of grace in the face of temptation? St Paul told those in Colossae:

> "As therefore you received Christ Jesus the Lord, so live in him, rooted and built up in him…see to it that no one makes a prey of you by philosophy and empty deceit, according to human tradition, according to the elemental spirits of the universe, and not according to Christ (Colossians 2:6-8)."

We must go to Christ, if we want to be built up in Him. Through our justification in Christ and our ongoing sanctification through the Holy Spirit, we can "boldly and confidently approach the throne of God's grace and receive grace and mercy (Hebrews 4:16)." God's mercy is limitless and His love is unconditional. He desires for us to know, have and seek His grace, so that we might live more in His image, in the image of the Incarnation.

It is by God's grace that we go from being slaves to being free (Romans 6:17-23). It is by God's grace that we move from death to life (Romans 6:13). It's by God's grace that you can make it through your day, each day. It's by God's grace that you go from living an ordinary life to living an extraordinary life. It's by God's grace that prayer becomes passionate, the Sacraments become intimate and Mary's heart was made immaculate. It's by God's grace that you can become a saint.

If you will work harder to protect your state of grace, move on to the next question. If you don't see the point, pray about it more before moving on.

10. Are you willing to share God's grace with *all* whom He puts before you?

God thinks more highly of you than you do of yourself. He believes in you. He believes in your potential. He doesn't just love you, God likes you; that's right, God *likes* you. He doesn't always like everything that you do, but He does like you. How do I know? Because He created you, uniquely and He redeemed you, personally.

God liked Saul, too, that's why God didn't give up on him, even when he was killing Christians. God remembers something that our fickle human brains always seem to forget…that He (God) can do more with a penitent sinner than He can a "saintly" person who doesn't feel they have any need of His mercy.

I am a sinner. So are you. I'm called to be a saint. So are you.
So, how do we do it? We don't…God's grace does.
All you have to do is let God be God…in you.

Sinners focus on self, saints on others.

Sinners focus on their wants, saints on what God wants.

Sinners, though, can and do become saints.

With the exception of the Blessed Virgin Mary, every saint began as a sinner.

Saints call out to sinners.

Saints are more aware of their sin than their saintliness.

Saints focus more on God's grace than their own sin.

Focus more on your "output" than your "input". Focus more on serving others than on how others can serve you. Remember the foot-washing at the Last Supper? You should remember it, every day. The more you seek Jesus in the Word, the Sacraments and prayer, the more you avail yourself of that Divine "input" the more power and grace you'll have to offer the world in your output. See how it works? St. Paul did. He served the body with every breath until his dying breath. That's how the sinner became the saint, He let God's life overtake his own life, and it overflowed onto every one God put in his path.

If you are willing to share God with *every one*, finish reading. If you are scared about sharing God with others, pray about it before moving on.

St. Paul Believes in Christ's Presence in You
You are beautiful and glorious and good. Even if you don't see Christ in yourself, you can bet that St. Paul would have seen and affirmed Christ in you! That's what the eyes of faith do, they see as God sees, not as man sees (1 Samuel 16:7). St. Paul would not only affirm your goodness but also remind you of how good you are designed to be.

He would never give up on you as others might do. He would never give up on you as you might have given up on yourself. Ask St. Paul to pray for you now.

St. Paul's intercessory prayer on your behalf is powerful. Ask him to join his prayers to your prayers as you lay them at the feet of Jesus Christ.

And believe in your goodness and in your holiness. Share that holiness with others and their hearts will, over time, be convicted to change, as well. Your example will call them to holiness in their own lives. Don't know how to "seek holiness?" It's simple, "seek first the Kingdom of God and His righteousness (Matthew 6:33)" in every decision, big and small. That is the challenge that makes life such an adventure. Make no mistake, you're not "choosing God", He already chose you (John 15:16)! God is calling you to respond.

St. Paul didn't just "see Christ" on the road one day. St. Paul, like countless saintly souls who came after him, saw Christ every day. He knew something that too many modern Christians (yes, even Catholics) proclaim but seem to forget, namely: Christ is living and active.

Christ's Word is living and active. His Sacraments and Church are living and active. And *you* are designed to be living *and* active, too. He created you to *live* not just to breathe…living in right relationship with God in the life of His Son (justification) and actively loving in power of His Spirit (sanctification).

So, as you turn this final page of text, consider how you, like St. Paul, might turn a new page of your walk with Christ, this day and, to quote our older brother in the faith one last time:

> "Put on then, as God's chosen ones, holy and beloved, compassion, kindness, lowliness, meekness, and patience, forbearing one another and, if one has a complaint against another, forgiving each other; as the Lord has forgiven you, so you also must forgive. And above all these put on love, which binds everything together in perfect harmony. And let the peace of Christ rule in your hearts, to which indeed you were called in the one body. And be thankful. Let the word of Christ dwell in you richly, teach and admonish one another in all wisdom, and sing psalms and hymns and spiritual songs with thankfulness in your hearts to God. And **whatever you do, in word or deed, do everything in the name of the Lord Jesus, giving thanks to God the Father through him** (Colossians 3:12-17)."

May the Spirit guide you on your adventure of life.

St. Paul, pray for us!

END NOTES

1 Peter Kreeft, *Reading and Praying the New Testament* (Ann Arbor, MI: Servant Books 1992) pg. 50.

2 Ronald Knox, *The Hidden Stream* (San Francisco, CA: Ignatius Press, 1953, 2003) pg. 96.

3 Richard John Neuhaus, "The Public Square," *First Things* 62, no. 181 (March 2008), www.firstthings.com/article.php3?id_article=6165.

4 Rev. Raneiro Cantalamessa, *Mary: Mirror of the Church* (The Liturgical Press: Collegeville, MN, 1992) pg. 17.

5 Walter Knight, *Knight's Master Book of 4000 Illustrations* (Grand Rapids, MI: Eerdmans) pgs. 235-236 and Hot Illustrations for Youth CD-ROM (Youth Speciaties, 2001).

6 Mark Hart, *Blessed are the Bored in Spirit: a Young Catholic's Search for Meaning* (Cincinnati, OH: Servant, 2006) p. 11.

7 Peter Kreeft, *Reading and Praying the New Testament* (Ann Arbor, MI: Servant Books, 1992) pgs. 73-74.

8 *Dominum et Vivificantem* ("The Holy Spirit in the Life of the Church and the World"), section 46. Emphasis his.

9 *Furrow*, no. 70 (http://www.escrivaworks.org/book/furrow-point-70.htm).

10 Paul Lee Tan, *Encyclopedia of 7700 illustrations* (Bible Comments, 1990).

11 Mark Hart & Todd Lemieux, *100 Things Every Catholic Teen Should Know* (Mesa, AZ: Life Teen, 2007) pg. 259.

12 Mark Hart, *Blessed are the Bored in Spirit: a Young Catholic's Search for Meaning* (Cincinnati, OH: Servant, 2006) p. 26.

13 *Then and Now Bible Maps* (Necedah,WI: Ascension Press, 1997) pgs. 13-15.

APPENDIX

TABLE OF CONTENTS

A CATECHETICAL STATEMENT
REGARDING CONTENT

A brief word to scholars…

As the subtitle suggests, this book is merely an introduction to the life and theology/teaching of St. Paul.

We are aware of the various issues and debate surrounding the "higher critical" approaches to the Pauline corpus in regards to composition, dating, background, and influence; but this book is not intended to weigh in on these controversies.

We are merely attempting to introduce some of the basic themes found within St. Paul's writings, and to offer a starting point for further research and edification.

It is our hope that the reader would find the preceding content and the following charts, outlines, summaries and maps, etc. to be helpful but not definitive in an ultimate or final sense.

United in the Holy Spirit,

Christopher Cuddy and Mark Hart

WHERE HE WENT

Wanna Go for a Walk?

Let's say that you live in Southern California. You're sitting out on the beach one day, just you and a couple of your friends. All of the sudden, in a flash of light, you have a vision of God. Jesus, Himself, is appearing to you and speaking to you. Your first inclination might be to apply heavier sunscreen or drink more water, fearing that you must be dehydrated, but the Living Water (John 7:37) is standing before you assuring you of His Divine presence. He assures you of your good-ness, His unconditional love for you and the eternal presence of His limitless mercy. He also tells you to stop sinning, for every time you sin against another, friend or foe, you sin against Him, your Savior.

Just then, He vanishes as quickly as He arrived and you make a divine promise. This won't be a "pact" or "covenant" like the others you've made and broken – the kind that begin with the phrase, "Lord, if you get me out of this, I promise I will…" No, this promise you actually intend to keep. You are so moved by the beauty of Jesus' message that you want to share this "good news" of His salvation and mercy with everyone you meet.

You immediately head home to pack up a couple outfits, an iPod, your Bible (ooh, you might need that), rosary, toothbrush and ATM card. You kiss your parents goodbye, shake a few hands and log off your mySpace account - for good. It's time to evangelize the world, for "evangelize" means to "share the gospel" and the gospel is the "good news" that Christ just made clear to you upon that beach. Is your next stop the airport or the bus station? Nice idea, but no. That's right, you don't own a car and you can't afford a plane ticket. Nope, it looks like you're going to have to make your way from San Diego to New York on foot.

What's the total distance of your trip? It's over 2400 miles.

Sure, you can go part of the way on horseback and by boat, if you're lucky. Of course, a boat won't help you get over the mountains in your path. You'll be stopping at several cities along the way; cities where people not only want nothing to do with you, but where you'll be threatened with death (and almost killed) for sharing the things you try to share with them about God's love and personal sins.

Would you still go?
Paul did.

He didn't evangelize because he wanted to make a name for himself. He already had a reputation, and it wasn't a good one with the people he was now supposed to call "family". Paul wasn't in it for the popularity, for the power, for the title or for the money…Paul went out and risked his life, every day, because the news he had received was *just that good*. He believed in it so deeply, that he stopped at nothing to preach it to the ends of the earth. What news was he spreading, what truth was he preaching? The truth contained in the gospels, printed in *your Bible*, sitting on *your nightstand* or *your coffee table*. The same words we utter out of habit, or read out of fear, or study filled with confusion, or recite with boredom are the words that kept his feet moving (for thousands of miles) around the ancient Mediterranean world.

According to the *Acts of the Apostles*, St. Paul's passport would have been stamped on just about every page.

Here's a rundown of where he went and *approximately* in what order:

Paul's missionary Tours

45-48	Paul's first journey (Galatia)
50-53	Paul's second journey (Greece)
53-58	Paul's third journey (Ephesus)
58	Paul in Jerusalem
58-60	Paul in Caesarea
60-61	Paul's fourth journey (to Rome)
61-63	Paul's first Roman captivity
67	Paul's second captivity
67	Paul executed

On the pages that follow you can see just how many cities Paul visited and just how many miles he traveled. The cities listed come straight from the *Acts of the Apostles* and the order confirmed by ancillary materials.[13]

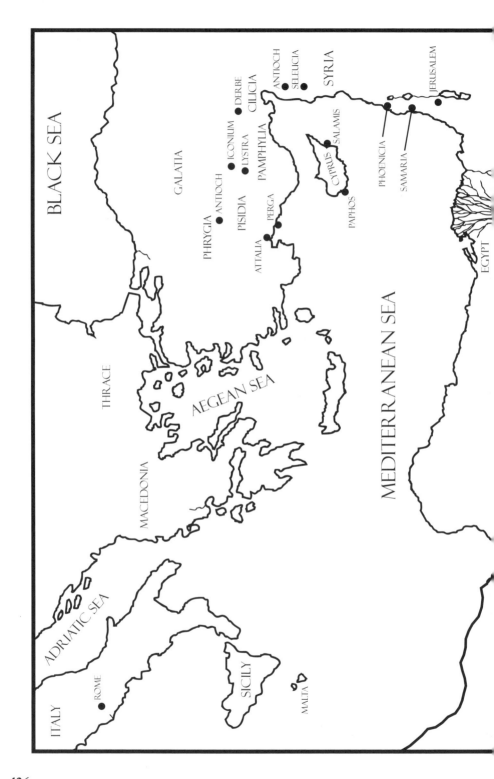

ST. PAUL'S FIRST MISSIONARY JOURNEY
ACTS 13:1-14:28

➤ ANTIOCH
➤ SELEUCIA
➤ SALAMIS AND PAPHOS (ON CYPRUS)
➤ PERGA
➤ ANTIOCH (OF PISIDIA)
➤ ICONIUM
➤ LYSTRA AND DERBE
➤ LYSTRA
➤ ICONIUM AND ANTIOCH
➤ PISIDIA, PAMPHYLIA, AND PERGA
➤ ATTALIA
➤ ANTIOCH
➤ JERUSALEM (VIA PHOENICIA AND SAMARIA)

TOTAL DISTANCE:
1500 MILES

TRAVELED WITH: BARNABAS, JOHN MARK

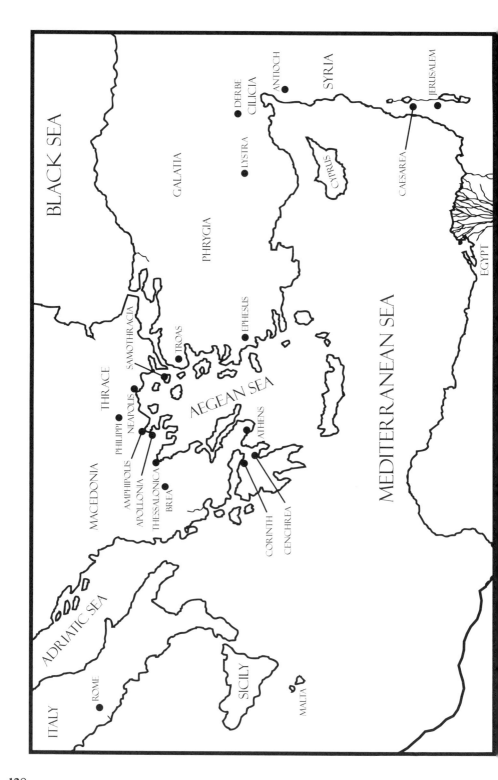

ST. PAUL'S SECOND MISSIONARY JOURNEY
ACTS 15:36-18:22

- ➤ SYRIA AND CILICIA
- ➤ DERBE AND LYSTRA
- ➤ PHRYGIA AND GALATIA
- ➤ TROAS
- ➤ SAMOTHRACIA AND NAPOLIS
- ➤ PHILIPPI IN MACEDONIA
- ➤ AMPHIPOLIS AND APOLLONIA
- ➤ THESSALONICA
- ➤ BEREA
- ➤ ATHENS (MARS HILL - "AREOPAGUS")
- ➤ CORINTH
- ➤ CENCHREA
- ➤ EPHEHSUS
- ➤ CAESAREA
- ➤ JERUSALEM
- ➤ ANTIOCH

TRAVELED WITH: SILAS, TIMOTHY, PRISCILLA, AQUILLA, LUKE

TOTAL DISTANCE:
2800 MILES

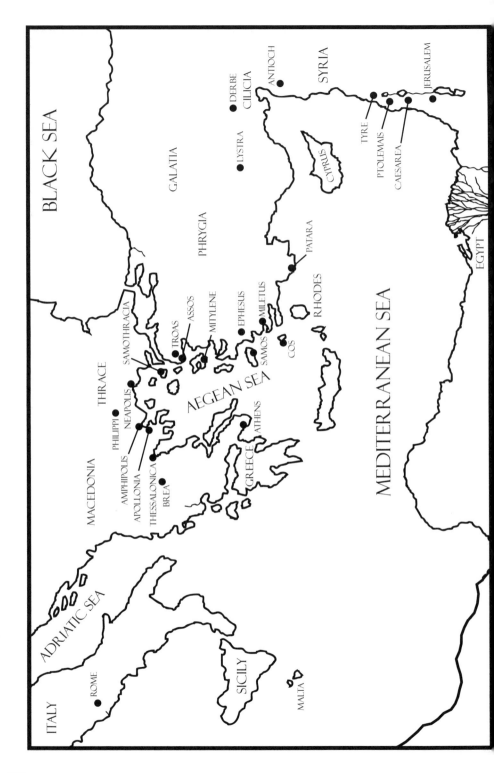

BLACK SEA

ANTIOCH

SYRIA

DERBE

CILICIA

JERUSALEM

LYSTRA

TYRE

PTOLEMAIS

CAESAREA

GALATIA

CYPRUS

PHRYGIA

PATARA

EGYPT

SAMOTHRACIA

TROAS

ASSOS

MITYLENE

EPHESUS

MILETUS

RHODES

THRACE

SAMOS

COS

MEDITERRANEAN SEA

PHILIPPI

NEAPOLIS

AEGEAN SEA

AMPHIPOLIS

APOLLONIA

THESSALONICA

BREA

ATHENS

MACEDONIA

GREECE

ITALY

ADRIATIC SEA

SICILY

ROME

MALTA

ST. PAUL'S THIRD MISSIONARY JOURNEY
ACTS 18:23-21:16

TOTAL DISTANCE:
2700 MILES

- ⋏ GALATIA AND PHRYGIA
- ⋏ EPHESUS
- ⋏ MACEDONIA
- ⋏ GREECE (ACHAIA)
- ⋏ MACEDONIA, PHILIPPI, AND TROAS
- ⋏ ASSOS, MITYLENE; NEAR CHIOS
- ⋏ SAMOS, (TROGYLLIUM), MILETUS
- ⋏ COS, PHODES, PATARA
- ⋏ TYRE AND PTOLEMAIS
- ⋏ CAESAREA
- ⋏ JERUSALEM

TRAVELED WITH: TIMOTHY, LUKE, OTHERS

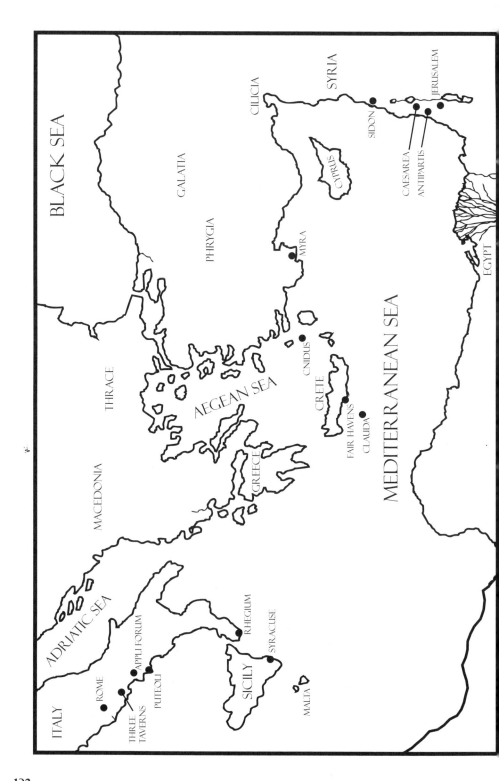

ST. PAUL'S JOURNEY TO ROME
ACTS 21:17-28:31

▲ JERUSALEM
▲ ANTIPATRIS AND CAESAREA
▲ SIDON, MYRA, CNIDUS
▲ FAIR HAVENS (CRETE)
▲ CLAUDA (CAUDA)
▲ MALTA (MELITA)
▲ SYRACUSE, RHEGIUM, PUTEOLI
▲ APPII FORUM, AND THREE TAVERNS
▲ ROME

TOTAL DISTANCE:
2300 MILES

TRAVELED WITH: ROMAN GUARDS, LUKE, OTHERS

WHAT HE WROTE

Introduction to the Writings of St. Paul

St. Paul was threatened by the elements, peers, imprisonment, death, and, ultimately, the Evil One, himself; yet he kept moving…and he kept writing.

On the pages that follow you will be given introductory information for personal and group Scripture study. While it is impossible to do justice to the inspired Word of God in just a couple of pages, these overviews — if prayerfully read and examined — could offer insights that may be profitable before, during and after you read St. Paul's writings.

Each overview will give you some central themes of the epistle, as well as some specific verses that are emblematic of the various points that St. Paul was making to his audiences.

Use the summaries as an introduction for private study. Use them in a group study as you begin to discuss the various overarching themes of each work. The point is this: use them. There is no reason to avoid St. Paul's writings. They are a beautiful gift from God and are meant to be explored. Prayerfully read through these sections in conjunction with the letters of St. Paul themselves, and watch how the second reading at Sunday Mass — and, most importantly, your soul — comes to life.

Romans

The letter of St. Paul to the Romans is a very special epistle. It displays the apostle's theological brilliance as well as his deep love and spirituality. It is St. Paul's longest and most influential letter.

St. Paul wrote the letter to introduce himself to the Christians who lived in the heavily populated city of Rome, and also to prepare them for his upcoming visit. The apostle had heard reports of trouble amidst the various Christian converts in the area. Through the ministry of the apostles, many people — both Jew and Gentile — came to faith in Christ. The converts changed their lives and fell madly in love with our Savior.

Unfortunately, however, problems arose. Some of the Jewish converts to Christianity believed that Jewish ceremonies like circumcision were still required before one could be a full member of the Church. Thus, some of the Jewish Christians were trying to force the Gentile Christians to get circumcised in addition to their Baptism. This provoked great controversy. Some thought that circumcision was still necessary, while others thought that Baptism was enough.

St. Paul's letter to the Romans is his authoritative answer to this issue: *only Baptism is required to be a Christian; circumcision is a sign of the Old Covenant, and it is unable to give the saving grace that Baptism gives.* Circumcision is not a sacrament. It is not required to be a follower of Christ. Baptism, as a Sacrament of faith, is sufficient.

Because this letter is so intricate and complicated, don't be discouraged if you find it to be pretty confusing at places. St. Paul deals with a lot of issues and themes that can become quite complex.

Here are some of the **key themes and verses** we discover in this letter:

• **The power of the Gospel:** "For I am not ashamed of the Gospel: it is the power of God for salvation to every one who has faith (Romans 1:16)."

• **Universal effect of sin:** "All have sinned and fall short of the glory of God (Romans 3:23)."

• **Faith, grace and salvation:** "Therefore, since we are justified by faith, we have peace with God through our Lord Jesus Christ. Through him we have obtained access to this grace in which we stand, and we rejoice in our hope of sharing the glory of God. More than that, we rejoice in our sufferings, knowing that suffering produces endurance, and endurance produces character, and character produces hope, and hope does not disappoint us, because God's love has been poured into our hearts through the Holy Spirit which has been given to us (Romans 5:1-5)."

• **Life through Christ:** "So you also must consider yourselves dead to sin and alive to God in Christ Jesus (Romans 6:11)."

• **Power of Baptism:** "Do you not know that all of us who have been baptized into Christ Jesus were baptized into his death? We were buried therefore with him by Baptism into death, so that as Christ was raised from the dead by the glory of the Father, we too might walk in newness of life (Romans 6:3-4)."

• **We are children of God:** "For all who are led by the Spirit of God are sons of God. For you did not receive the spirit of slavery to fall back into fear, but you have received the spirit of sonship. When we cry, 'Abba! Father!' it is the Spirit himself bearing witness with our spirit that we are children of God, and if children, then heirs, heirs of God and fellow heirs with Christ, provided we suffer with him in order that we may also be glorified with him (Romans 8:14-17)."

• **God's sovereign purpose:** "We know that in everything God works for good with those who love him, who are called according to his purpose (Romans 8:28)."

• **Christian transformation:** "Do not be conformed to this world but be transformed by the renewal of your mind, that you may prove what is the will of God, what is good and acceptable and perfect (Romans 12:2)."

First and Second Corinthians

The city of Corinth was a busy place. A lot of trading was done in the city, and it was known for its great economic prosperity and success. Attracting many people from all walks of life, Corinth was also known for its rampant sinfulness. It was kind of like the Las Vegas of its time.

St. Paul himself had helped to start the Church in Corinth, but he was unable to remain in the city and oversee its spiritual growth (Acts 18:1-18). Unfortunately, a lot of scandalous behavior began to emerge within the Church in Corinth after the apostle left. Through word of mouth, St. Paul heard about some of the gross sins the Christians had been committing, and he was writing to encourage them to reject their immoral behavior and to renew their commitment to a life grounded in the love of Christ (1 Corinthians 10:6-13).

First and Second Corinthians are very powerful letters, and they address a lot of the struggles we face in the Christian life. Peer pressure isn't something new. It is something that Christians living in the early Church had to face as well. And in these letters St. Paul is very understanding and sensitive to human weakness, yet clear about how we should respond to struggles in the Christian life. Like a good father, St. Paul is lovingly firm in his guidance (2 Corinthians 10-13). He reminds us that everything we have — even our bodies — belongs to Christ (1 Corinthians 6:12-20), and that we should pursue love above all things (1 Corinthians 12-14).

The Christian life is not easy, but Christ's love and grace are sufficient to get us through the difficult times and overcome our weaknesses (2 Corinthians 8-10).

Here are some of the **key themes and verses** we discover in these letters:

• **Christian unity and maturity are very important:** "I appeal to you, brethren, by the name of our Lord Jesus Christ, that all of you agree and that there be no dissensions among you, but that you be united in the same mind and the same judgment (1 Corinthians 1:10-4:21)."

• **Marriage and celibacy are both sacred callings, and they should be treasured:** "I wish that all were as I myself am. But each has his own special gift from God, one of one kind and one of another (1 Corinthians 7)."

• **The Eucharist is sacred and must be treated with great reverence:** "Whoever, therefore, eats the bread or drinks the cup of the Lord in an unworthy manner will be guilty of profaning the body and blood of the Lord. Let a man examine himself, and so eat of the bread and drink of the cup. For any one who eats and drinks without discerning the body eats and drinks judgment upon himself (1 Corinthians 11:23-32)."

• **Love is the greatest of all spiritual gifts:** "So faith, hope, love abide, these three; but the greatest of these is love (1 Corinthians 12-14)."

• **Christ will comfort us in our suffering:** "For as we share abundantly in Christ's sufferings, so through Christ we share abundantly in comfort too (2 Corinthians 1:3-14)."

• **Christ has transformed us by the power of His love:** "Therefore, if any one is in Christ, he is a new creation; the old has passed away, behold the new has come (2 Corinthians 5-6)."

• **Be generous to God and those around you:** "He who sows sparingly will also reap sparingly, and he who sows bountifully will also reap bountifully (2 Corinthians 8-9)."

• **God can overcome every human weakness:** "'My grace is sufficient for you, for my power is made perfect in weakness.' I will all the more gladly boast in my weaknesses, that the power of Christ may rest upon me...for when I am weak, then I am strong (2 Corinthians 10-13)."

Galatians

Although not quite as long (or as complicated) as his epistle to the Romans, the letter of St. Paul to the Galatians is also focused on this primary question: *Does one have to be circumcised in order to be a full Christian?* Again, as he said in Romans, the answer is *no*. Circumcision is not necessary. It does not communicate grace. Baptism — not circumcision — communicates grace and enters us into God's covenant family.

St. Paul is writing to persuade Christians that the ceremonial laws and practices of the old covenant are no longer necessary. In fact, they are now harmful. Through the person and work of Jesus Christ, the Old Covenant ceremonies ("works of the law" like circumcision, diet restrictions and animal sacrifices) are retired. Jesus set us free from these ceremonial practices of the old covenant. Returning to them would be to reject the work of Christ and would do great spiritual damage.

Before Jesus came, circumcision was the way in which someone entered God's covenant community (Leviticus 12:3). However, the life, death and resurrection of Jesus brought about a *New Covenant* which is much more powerful and will never end. In Jesus we are set free from the Old Covenant curses (Galatians 3:13) and have become a "new creation" in Christ (Galatians 6:15). Jesus' work fulfilled the old covenant and established the new covenant of faith (Galatians 3:7) entered by way of Baptism (Galatians 3:27). This new covenant is much more personal than the old. Through Jesus Christ we have become adopted children of God (Galatians 4:1-7).

The important thing to focus on in this letter is the centrality of Jesus in everything. Jesus is our salvation. He gave up His human life in order that we might receive His divine life. Through Baptism we become God's divinely adopted sons and daughters. Christ gave us infinitely more than we could ever deserve or imagine. Prayerfully read through this epistle, stopping to thank God along the way for all of the many blessings and gifts you see the apostle identify in its pages.

Here are some of the key themes and verses we discover in this letter:

• **Faith in Christ is the key to salvation:** "Man is not justified by works of the law [i.e. circumcision] but through faith in Jesus Christ (Galatians 2:16)."

• **Baptism unites us to Christ:** "In Christ Jesus you are all sons of God, through faith. For as many of you as were baptized into Christ have put on Christ (Galatians 3:26-27)."

• **Jesus was sent into the world to make us divinely adopted sons and daughters:** "God sent forth his Son, born of woman, born under the law, to redeem those who were under the law, so that we might receive adoption as sons. And because you are sons, God has sent the Spirit of his Son into our hearts, crying, 'Abba! Father!' So through God you are no longer a slave but a son, and if a son then an heir (Galatians 4:4-7)."

• **Faith and love are the key to the Christian life:** "For in Christ Jesus neither circumcision nor uncircumcision is of any avail, but faith working through love (Galatians 5:6)."

• **Jesus made us free in order to love:** "For you were called to freedom, brethren; only do not use your freedom as an opportunity for the flesh, but through love be servants of one another (Galatians 5:13)."

• **The "Fruits of the Spirit":** "The fruit of the Spirit is love, joy, peace, patience, kindness, goodness, faithfulness, gentleness, self-control (Galatians 5:22-23)."

• **Living in the Spirit:** "If we live by the Spirit, let us also walk by the Spirit. Let us have no self-conceit, no provoking of one another, no envy of one another Galatians 5:25-26)."

• **Care for others:** "Bear one another's burdens, and so fulfill the law of Christ (Galatians 6:2)."

• **Don't lose hope when things grow difficult:** "Let us not grow weary in well-doing, for in due season we shall reap, if we do not lose heart. So then, as we have opportunity, let us do good to all men, and especially to those who are of the household of faith (Galatians 6:9-10)."

Ephesians

The "mystery" of Jesus Christ is both the key to our salvation and the central theme in St. Paul's letter to the Ephesians (Ephesians 1:9; 3:4, 9). The mystery of Christ has various dimensions. Jesus is the Savior of the world, and he came to die on the cross for the sins of all people — no matter what their background of former way of life. After his death and resurrection, Jesus ascended into Heaven where He is highly exalted and is seated at the right hand of the Father (Ephesians 1:20-23).

St. Paul spends a lot of time going through these things because he believes that they are vitally important in our lives today. Although they occurred in the past, Christ's life, death and resurrection continue to have power and relevance in the modern period. Even though Jesus isn't currently walking the earth in bodily form, His presence is still real and powerful through the life and ministry of the Church — in fact, the two are joined together (Ephesians 5:32). The Church isn't optional. It is a necessary part of Christ's lasting gift to his people. Christ is the "head" and center of the Church, and it is He who unites the Church (Ephesians 5:23).

This letter is St. Paul's attempt to help his readers more fully understand the profound graces they have received from God in and through Jesus and His Church. As you read this, meditate on the blessings you have received through the sacraments, and look for advice from the apostle about how to live out your divine sonship.

Here are some of the **key themes and verses** we discover in this letter:

• **God chose us to be his children before the world was created:** "He chose us in him before the foundation of the world, that we should be holy and blameless before him. He destined us in love to be his sons through Jesus Christ according to the purpose of his will, to the praise of his glorious grace which he freely bestowed on us in the Beloved (Ephesians 1:4-6)."

• **God's "mysterious plan" was to bring us home to Him:** "He has made known to us the mystery of his will, according to his purpose which he set forth in Christ as a plan for the fullness of time, to unite all things in him, thing in heaven and things on earth (Ephesians 1:9-10)."

• **God's love and mercy are the reasons for our salvation:** "God, who is rich in mercy, out of the great love with which he loved us, even when we were dead through our trespasses, made us alive together with Christ (by grace you have been saved), and raised us up to him, and made us sit with him in the heavenly places in Christ Jesus (Ephesians 2:4-6)."

• **Salvation by grace through faith:** "For by grace you have been saved through faith; and this is not your own doing, it is the gift of God — not because of works, lest any man should boast (Ephesians 2:8-9)."

• **Unity in the Spirit:** "There is one body and one Spirit, just as you were called to the one hope that belongs to your call, one Lord, one faith, one Baptism, one God and Father of us all, who is above all and through all and in all (Ephesians 4:4-6)."

• **The imitation of Christ:** "Be imitators of God, as beloved children. And walk in love, as Christ loved us and gave himself up for us, a fragrant offering and sacrifice to God (Ephesians 5:1-2)."

• **We need the truth and love of Christ to win the battle for our souls:** "Take the whole armor of God, that you may be able to withstand in the evil day, and having done all, to stand (Ephesians 6:13-18)."

Philippians

The letter of St. Paul to the Philippians is an epistle of encouragement and thanksgiving. The Church in Philippi was always eager to support the work of Christ no matter what the cost, and the apostle wants to express his profound gratitude for their prayers and assistance. This is a very personal letter from the pen of St. Paul. Unlike his letters to the Romans and the Galatians, there are no big debates or controversies to be resolved. Thus, Philippians is also rather informal in style — in a way similar to how we could write close friends.

The apostle encourages his readers to follow his example of imitating Jesus in all things, but especially in terms of his *servanthood* (Philippians 2:1-11; 2:12-18). St. Paul is committed to his Savior in all and through all. The Christian life is not easy, but the apostle Paul is adamant about the fact that the joy of knowing Christ is worth every struggle.

As you read through this short epistle, look for ways you can imitate St. Paul's servanthood and more fully receive the joy of knowing Jesus in your own life.

Here are some of the **key themes and verses** we discover in this letter:

• **Love Jesus in all things:** "With full courage now as always Christ will be honored in my body, whether by life or by death. For to me to live is Christ, and to die is gain (Philippians 1:20-21)."

• **Suffering is a part of the Christian life:** "It has been granted to you that for the sake of Christ you should not only believe in him but also suffer for his sake (Philippians 1:29)."

• **Christ was the supreme servant:** "[Though Jesus] was in the form of God, did not count equality with God something to be grasped, but emptied himself, taking the form of a servant, being born in the likeness of men…he humbled himself and became obedient unto death…Therefore God has highly exalted him (Philippians 2:5-11)."

• **Nothing compares to the joy found in knowing Christ Jesus:** "But whatever gain I had, I counted as loss for the sake of Christ. Indeed I count everything as loss because of the surpassing worth of knowing Christ Jesus my Lord. For his sake I have suffered the loss of all things, and count them as refuse, in order that I might gain Christ (Philippians 3:7-11)."

• **Our real home is in Heaven with Jesus:** "Our commonwealth is in heaven, and from it we await a Savior, the Lord Jesus Christ, who will change our lowly body to be like his glorious body (Philippians 3:20-21)."

• **Only in Jesus will we find eternal joy and happiness:** "Rejoice in the Lord always; again I will say, Rejoice…the peace of God, which passes all understanding will keep your hearts and your minds in Christ Jesus (Philippians 4:4-7)."

• **The "focuses" of the Christian life:** ""Finally, brethren, whatever is true, whatever is honorable, whatever is just, whatever is pure, whatever is lovely, whatever is gracious, if there is any excellence, if there is anything worthy of praise, think about these things (Philippians 4:8)."

Colossians

The letter of St. Paul to the Colossians is an interesting epistle. Unlike some of the others, St. Paul did not personally found or visit the Church in Colossae (Colossians 2:1). St. Paul had heard about the Colossian Church through a man named Epaphras (Colossians 1:7; 4:12) who informed the apostle about the struggles of this young Christian community.

Apparently some rabble-rousers were attempting to persuade people that the faith of the Gentile Christians was inadequate. The Jews of the time were very critical of the Gentile converts because they were uncircumcised. Again, St. Paul reiterates the fact that circumcision is a sign of the Old Covenant, and it is no longer necessary because of Christ's death and resurrection. He is very pastoral in his tone, and reassures the Gentile Christians that they are full-fledged members of God's covenantal family by way of faith and Baptism (Colossians 1:21-23; 2:11-12).

St. Paul stresses the fact Jesus Christ is at the center of reality and that he should be at the center of our lives. Christ reigns supreme. He is almighty overall and over all. God is sovereign. Nothing escapes His influence, authority and power. And while there is opposition to Christ and his Church, the battle is as good as won. Christ has triumphed over all opposing forces (Colossians 2:15-23).

Because he is supreme, Christ is sufficient for our every need. Through Baptism we are united to Christ (Colossians 2:12), and in Christ we encounter the fullness of life, love and salvation. Hence, we should strive to conform our lives to the saving Gospel of Jesus Christ. We must be vigilant in our prayer and commitment to the grace of Christ, for in it we find our strength and power (Colossians 4:2).

As you read this epistle, meditate on the various passages which refer to the supremacy of Jesus and think of ways you can give glory to Him through your words and actions.

Here are some of the **key themes and verses** we discover in this letter:

• **Christ is central and supreme:** "[Christ] is the image of the invisible God, the first born of all creation; for in him all things were created (Colossians 1:15-20)."

• **Our suffering unites us to Christ and aids the Church:** "I rejoice in my sufferings for your sake, and in my flesh I complete what is lacking in Christ's afflictions for the sake of his body, that is, the church (Colossians 1:24-25)."

• **We must be heavenly minded:** "Set your minds on things that are above, not on things which are on earth…your life is hid with Christ in God (Colossians 3:2-4)."

• **Love must be central:** "Above all these put on love, which binds everything together in perfect harmony (Colossians 3:12-17)."

• **Whatever we do should be done for the glory of God:** "Whatever your task, work heartily, as serving the Lord and not men, knowing that from the Lord you will receive the inheritance as your reward; you are serving the Lord Christ (Colossians 3:23-24)."

First and Second Thessalonians

The letters of St. Paul to the Thessalonians are very pastoral. The apostle is writing to a group of recent converts who are experiencing great persecution. He offers his prayers, thoughts and paternal encouragement in their time of great trial and difficulty. He commends them for their growth faith, hope and love (1 Thessalonians 1:3; 3:6; 5:8), offers no big criticisms or reprimands, and urges them to remain steady in the Christian journey (1 Thessalonians 4:1; 5:11).

As in all his epistles, the apostle urges his readers to be vigilant in love (1 Thessalonians 3:12) and holiness (1 Thessalonians 3:13; 5:23). He reminds them that Jesus will one day return in glory to save us from wrath and give us salvation (1 Thessalonians 1:10; 5:9; 2 Thessalonians 1:10). No one knows when Jesus will return and that is why we must remain steadfast at all times, ready for his arrival (1 Thessalonians 5:1-11). He offers great hope to his readers, assuring them that those in Christ will be escorted to the glory of Heaven just like Jesus himself had been carried to Heaven (1 Thessalonians 4:14-18).

Here are some of the **key themes and verses** we discover in this letter:

• **God chooses His people:** "For we know, brethren beloved by God, that he has chosen you (1 Thessalonians 1:4; 2 Thessalonians 2:13)."

• **Pursue holiness and flee immorality:** "For this is the will of God, your sanctification: that you abstain from immorality; that each one of you knows how to control his own body in holiness and honor (1 Thessalonians 4:3-8)."

• **All who die in the love of Christ will rise again in glory:** "For since we believe that Jesus died and rose again, even so, through Jesus, God will bring with him those who have fallen asleep…the dead in Christ will rise (1 Thessalonians 4:13-17; 2 Thessalonians 1:10-12)."

• **Until Christ returns, be vigilant in faith, hope and love:** "Let us be sober, and put on the breastplate of faith and love, and for a helmet the hope of salvation (1 Thessalonians 5:8-11)."

• **Do not depart from the teachings and guidance of the Church:** "Stand firm and hold to the traditions which you were taught by us, either by word of mouth or by letter (2 Thessalonians 2:15, 3:6)."

First and Second Timothy

The letters of St. Paul to Timothy are unique among the apostle's writings. Timothy was stationed in the Church at Ephesus in order to help it recover from the damage of some false teachers who had been deceiving God's people (1 Timothy 1:3-7; 6:3-5).

In a very loving way, the apostle encourages Timothy to remain firm in the truth (1 Timothy 4:6-7; 6:20). Sound doctrine is important. St. Paul is adamant about the fact that God's people must be taught nothing less than the fullness of truth (2 Timothy 1:13-14; 4:2-3). As a spiritual mentor, St. Paul encourages Timothy to continue preaching the Gospel message of Jesus Christ long after the apostle has passed on to the next life (2 Timothy 4:6-8). Following Christ is not an easy task, but the apostle urges Timothy to take courage and strength from his example of faithfulness (2 Timothy 3:10-14).

St. Paul instructs his young friend to "guard" the truth of the Gospel (2 Timothy 1:14). The truth of God is sacred. It is not to be modified or adjusted to fit the trivial preferences of mere humans (2 Timothy 4:3-5).

Here are some of the **key themes and verses** we discover in this letter:

• **The one God and Mediator:** "There is one God, and there is one mediator between God and men, the man Christ Jesus who gave himself as a ransom for all (1 Timothy 2:5-6)."

• **The Church is a pillar of truth:** "The church of the living God, [is] the pillar and bulwark of the truth (1 Timothy 2:15)."

• **God doesn't make junk:** "For everything created by God is good, and nothing is to be rejected if it is received with thanksgiving (1 Timothy 4:4)."

• **Christians should care for one another:** "If any one does not provide for his relatives, and especially for his own family, he has disowned the faith and is worse than an unbeliever (1 Timothy 5:8)."

• **Fight for the truth and holiness:** "Aim at righteousness, godliness, faith, love, steadfastness, gentleness. Fight the good fight of the faith (1 Timothy 6:11)."

• **Confidence in Christ:** "I am not ashamed, for I know whom I have believed, and I am sure that he is able to guard until that Day what has been entrusted to me (2 Timothy 1:12)."

• **Scripture is sacred and inspired by God Himself:** "All scripture is inspired by God and profitable for teaching, for reproof, for correction, and for training in righteousness, that the man of God may be complete, equipped for every good work (2 Timothy 3:16-17)."

Titus

Titus and St. Paul had worked together to evangelize parts of the Island of Crete. When the apostle left Crete to go spread the saving message of Jesus to other places, Titus remained to organize the Christian converts and help them form a solid community.

Like his letters to Timothy, St. Paul is very pastoral in his advice and counsel to Titus. He exhorts Titus to remain firm in the unwavering truth of Christ (Titus 1:10-16; 2:1). The apostle also spends time giving Titus advice about how discern which men are worthy to be ordained to the priesthood (Titus 1:5). Because the call to priesthood (i.e. to be an "elder") is a sacred vocation, this discernment should be done very carefully. St. Paul instructs Titus to evaluate a candidate's character and family when considering someone for ordination (Titus 1:7-8). The reason for this is simple: people will learn about Christ through the lifestyle and actions of Christian leaders. Holy leaders will do much to further Christ's kingdom. Poor leaders will do much to hinder the cause of Christ. Spirit-led discernment and wisdom are essential.

While this is especially true for priests and bishops, it is true for all Christians. St. Paul reminds Titus that all believers should be faithful and holy in word and action (Titus 2:7; 3:1-14). We are called to be Christ to all people whether they are fellow Christians or not (Titus 2:2-10; 3:1-2).

Here are some of the **key themes and verses** we discover in this letter:

• **We can have great confidence in the saving promises of God:** "Paul, a servant of God and an apostle of Jesus Christ, to further the faith of God's elect and their knowledge of the truth which accords with godliness, in hope of eternal life which God, who never lies, promised ages ago (Titus 1:1-3)."

• **Pursue holiness in all things:** "Show yourself in all respects a model of good deeds, and in your teaching show integrity, gravity, and sound speech (Titus 2:7)."

• **Avoid mean-spirited interactions:** "Speak evil of no one…avoid quarreling (Titus 3:2)."

• **The grace of Christ is the key to salvation:** "[Christ] saved us, not because of deeds done by us in righteousness, but in virtue of his own mercy, by the washing of regeneration and renewal in the Holy Spirit, which he poured out upon us richly through Jesus Christ our Savior, so that we might be justified by his grace and become heirs in hope of eternal life (Titus 2:5-7)."

Philemon

The letter of St. Paul to Philemon is the shortest epistle from the pen of St. Paul. This is a moving letter that gives a very intimate glimpse into the heart of the apostle Paul. It is written to a slave owner named Philemon, a woman named Apphia (possibly Philemon's wife), and a man named Archippus (possibly Philemon's son). St. Paul wrote this letter requesting that Philemon welcome back one of his runaway slaves (a man named Onesimus).

Apparently, Onesimus had originally been "useless" and unfaithful to his master, perhaps even stealing from Philemon (Philemon 1:11, 18). However, God's grace is powerful and it seems that Onesimus had a conversion to Christ through the ministry of St. Paul. The apostle sent Onesimus back to his master (Philemon 1:12), and wrote to Philemon encouraging him to embrace Onesimus as a brother in Christ (Philemon 1:16).

This epistle, though short, is a beautiful glimpse into true Christian conversion, love, mercy and forgiveness. As you read it, meditate on the power of God's loving mercy and forgiveness to transform every part of our life and being.

A PLAN FOR READING THE SCRIPTURES WITH ST. PAUL

We want to know Christ as intimately as St. Paul knew him. We want you to know Christ that intimately, too. We are going to give you two "plans" on how to dive more deeply into the Holy Spirit's Words from St. Paul. Plan A involves working back through this book, again, reading and journaling along with St. Paul's Letter to the Romans at the same time. Plan B involves reading through St. Paul's letters in the (proposed) order of their composition, offering you a look into the evolution of his discipleship and ministry.

Either plan is sure to challenge and bless you, because anytime you open yourself up to God and make time to study His Word, His grace is there in abundance. Ask St. Paul, now, to pray with you and for you as you journey deeper into the mind and heart of Christ through His Word and through the words contained here. St. Paul's prayerful intercession, as with all the saints, is powerful and valuable in our walk with and to Christ.

Plan A
Read through Romans (right hand) and this book in your left.

You'll notice a consistency and flow:

Romans	*Sword of the Spirit*
Romans 1-2	Chapter 1
Romans 3-4	Chapter 2
Romans 5-6	Chapter 3
Romans 7-11	Chapter 4
Romans 12-14	Chapter 5
Romans 14-16	Chapter 6

Plan B
Read through St. Paul's writings in order of their composition.

While we are not absolutely certain as to the order of composition, there is a generally held belief among most Bible scholars as to the basic timeline of St. Paul's travel and writings. As we stated earlier, we're going to work off of the following proposed timeline of composition:

Pauline Letters in order of composition

50-51	1 Thessalonians (written from Corinth)
50-51	2 Thessalonians (written from Corinth)
56	1 Corinthians (written from Ephesus)
53-57	Galatians (written from Phillipi)
56	2 Corinthians (written from Phillipi)
54-58	Philippians
57-58	Romans (from Corinth)
60-62	Ephesians
60-62	Colossians
60-62	Philemon
63-67	1 Timothy (between captivities)
63-67	Titus (between captivities)
63-67	2 Timothy

How long will it take to read them in this order? How should you go about it? How about one chapter a day? In that time, you could read through all of St. Paul's works in 87 days...*less than 3 months.*

1 Thessalonians	(5 chapters)
2 Thessalonians	(3 chapters)
1 Corinthians	(16 chapters)
Galatians	(6 chapters)
2 Corinthians	(13 chapters)
Philippians	(4 chapters)
Romans	(16 chapters)
Ephesians	(6 chapters)
Colossians	(4 chapters)
Philemon	(1 chapter)
1 Timothy	(6 chapters)
Titus	(3 chapters)
2 Timothy	(4 chapters)

If you read the writings in this order you are bound to see an evolution in the heart of St. Paul, one that ends in total humility and emptiness to this world, but fullness in Christ. You'll also notice a truth that is at the heart of St. Paul's writing(s) throughout: conversion is not a one-time occurrence. True conversion of heart is an ongoing surrender to God's will and Christ's mercy.

INTRODUCTION TO THE CYCLE OF SUNDAY READINGS

The Roman Catholic Church is very intentional and quite wise. She gives us an incredible gift in the assembly of the Sacred Scriptures we proclaim and hear at every Mass. Basically, the Church puts the Scriptures into what are called "cycles".

The Mass readings are taken directly out of the Bible and put into two "cycles", one for weekdays and one for Sundays. The cycle insures that we receive the fullness of God's Divine revelation in a systematic and intentional way.

The cycle for Sunday is divided into three "years' worth" of readings, A, B and C.
Year A focuses mainly on the Gospel of St. Matthew
Year B focuses mainly on the Gospel of St. Mark (and John chapter 6)
Year C focuses mainly on the Gospel of St. Luke.

During Easter season each year, we hear mainly from the Gospel of St. John. The cycles change on the 1st Sunday of Advent (not January 1st) because Advent is the beginning of the liturgical year. One the pages that follow you will find the three "cycles" of Sunday readings. Take advantage of them!

The cycle we are "in" depends on the calendar year.
Cycle A – 2008, 2011, 2014, 2017
Cycle B – 2009, 2012, 2015, 2018
Cycle C – 2010, 2013, 2016, 2019

Take the time to read and pray through them ahead of time and you will be amazed at how your experience during the Liturgy of the Word (the first half of Mass) comes to life in a new way. If you're wondering "what Sunday are we on or which one is coming up?" just check your parish bulletin, it's usually listed inside the front cover.

You'll notice that at each Sunday Mass we have three readings and a Psalm response – making four Scriptural texts. They are "grouped together" and compiled that way for a reason. When you read and pray through them, you'll find (if you read closely enough) that they have a "strand" or a "theme" that ties them all together.

Check out Life Teen's "Sunday Sunday Sunday" podcast (available through iTunes or on the www.lifeteen.com) to see how the Sunday readings work together each week, to lead us closer to Christ.

Getting more out of Mass is as easy as reading ahead. It's as simple as A, B, C…

CYCLE A

Cycle of Sunday readings
2011, 2014, 2017

Advent Season
1st Sunday of Advent
  1- Isa 2:1-5
  2- Rom 13:11-14
  3- Mt 24:37-44

2nd Sunday of Advent
  1- Isa 11:1-10
  2- Rom 15:4-9
  3- Mt 3:1-12

3rd Sunday of Advent
  1- Isa 35:1-6a,10
  2- Jms 5:7-10
  3- Mt 11:2-11

4th Sunday of Advent
  1- Isa 7:10-14
  2- Rom 1:1-7
  3- Mt 1:18-24

Christmas Season
Christmas Vigil
  1- Isa 62:1-5
  2- Acts 13:16-17,22-25
  3- Mt 1:1-25

Christmas (At Midnight)
  1- Isa 9:1-6
  2- Ti 2:11-14
  3- Lk 2:1-14

Christmas (At Dawn)
  1- Isa 62:11-12
  2- Ti 3:4-7
  3- Lk 2:15-20

Christmas (During the Day)
  1- Isa 52:7-10
  2- Heb 1:1-6
  3- Jn 1:1-18

Sunday After Christmas
(Holy Family)
  1- Sirach 3:2-6,12-14
  2- Col 3:12-21
  3- Mt 2:13-15,19-23

January 1
(Solemnity of Mary, Mother of God)
  1- Num 6:22-27
  2- Gal 4:4-7
  3- Lk 2:16-21

2nd Sunday After Christmas
  1- Sirach 24:1-2,8-12
  2- Eph 1:3-6,15-18
  3- Jn 1:1-18

Epiphany
  1- Isa 60:1-6
  2- Eph 3:2-3a,5-6
  3- Mt 2:1-12

Sunday After Epiphany
(Baptism of the Lord)
  1- Isa 42:1-4,6-7
  2- Acts 10:34-38
  3- Mt 3:13-17

Lenten Season
Ash Wednesday
  1- Joel 2:12-18
  2- 2Cor 5:20--6:2
  3- Mt 6:1-6,16-18

1st Sunday of Lent
  1- Gen 2:7-9; 3:1-7
  2- Rom 5:12-19
  3- Mt 4:1-11

2nd Sunday of Lent
  1- Gen 12:1-4a
  2- 2Tm 1:8b-10
  3- Mt 17:1-9

3rd Sunday of Lent
  1- Ex 17:3-7
  2- Rom 5:1-2,5-8
  3- Jn 4:5-42

4th Sunday of Lent
  1- 1Sam 16:1b,6-7,10-13a
  2- Eph 5:8-14
  3- Jn 9:1-41

5th Sunday of Lent
  1- Ezek 37:12-14
  2- Rom 8:8-11
  3- Jn 11:1-45

Passion Sunday (Palm Sunday)
Procession: Mt 21:1-11
  1- Isa 50:4-7
  2- Phil 2:6-11
  3- Mt 26:14--27:66

Easter Triduum & Easter Season
  1- Isa 61:1-3a,6a,8b-9
  2- Rev 1:5-8
  3- Lk 4:16-21

Mass of Lord's Supper
  1- Ex 12:1-8,11-14
  2- 1Cor 11:23-26
  3- Jn 13:1-15

Good Friday
  1- Isa 52:13--53:12
  2- Heb 4:14-16; 5:7-9
  3- Jn 18:1--19:42

Easter Vigil
  1- Gen 1:1--2:2
  Gen 22:1-18
  Ex 14:15--15:1
  Isa 54:5-14
  Isa 55:1-11
  Baruch 3:9-15,32--4:4
  Ezek 36:16-28
  2- Rom 6:3-11
  3- Mt 28:1-10

Easter Sunday
  1- Acts 10:34a,37-43
  2- Col 3:1-4
  or 1Cor 5:6b-8
  3- Jn 20:1-9
  or Mt 28:1-10
  Evening: 3- Lk 24:13-35

2nd Sunday of Easter
  1- Acts 2:42-47
  2- 1Pt 1:3-9
  3- Jn 20:19-31

3rd Sunday of Easter
1- Acts 2:14,22-28
2- 1Pt 1:17-21
3- Lk 24:13-35

4th Sunday of Easter
1- Acts 2:14a,36-41
2- 1Pt 2:20b-25
3- Jn 10:1-10

5th Sunday of Easter
1- Acts 6:1-7
2- 1Pt 2:4-9
3- Jn 14:1-12

6th Sunday of Easter
1- Acts 8:5-8,14-17
2- 1Pt 3:15-18
3- Jn 14:15-21

Ascension of Our Lord
1- Acts 1:1-11
2- Eph 1:17-23
3- Mt 28:16-20

7th Sunday of Easter
1- Acts 1:12-14
2- 1Pt 4:13-16
3- Jn 17:1-11a

Pentecost Vigil
1- Gen 11:1-9
or Ex 19:3-8a,16-20b
or Ezek 37:1-14
or Joel 3:1-5
2- Rom 8:22-27
3- Jn 7:37-39

Mass of the Day
1- Acts 2:1-11
2- 1Cor 12:3b-7,12-13
3- Jn 20:19-23

Solemnities of the Lord During Ordinary Time
Trinity Sunday
(Sunday after Pentecost)
1- Ex 34:4b-6,8-9
2- 2Cor 13:11-13
3- Jn 3:16-18

Corpus Christi
1- Deut 8:2-3,14b-16a
2- 1Cor 10:16-17
3- Jn 6:51-58

Sacred Heart of Jesus
1- Deut 7:6-11
2- 1Jn 4:7-16
3- Mt 11:25-30

Ordinary Time
1st Sunday
(See Baptism of the Lord, above)
2nd Sunday
1- Isa 49:3,5-6
2- 1Cor 1:1-3
3- Jn 1:29-34

3rd Sunday
1- Isa 8:23b--9:3
2- 1Cor 1:10-13,17
3- Mt 4:12-23

4th Sunday
1- Zeph 2:3; 3:12-13
2- 1Cor 1:26-31
3- Mt 5:1-12a

5th Sunday
1- Isa 58:7-10
2- 1Cor 2:1-5
3- Mt 5:13-16

6th Sunday
1- Sirach 15:15-20
2- 1Cor 2:6-10
3- Mt 5:17-37

7th Sunday
1- Lev 19:1-2,17-18
2- 1Cor 3:16-23
3- Mt 5:38-48

8th Sunday
1- Isa 49:14-15
2- 1Cor 4:1-5
3- Mt 6:24-34

9th Sunday
1- Deut 11:18,26-28
2- Rom 3:21-25a,28
3- Mt 7:21-27

10th Sunday
1- Hosea 6:3-6
2- Rom 4:18-25
3- Mt 9:9-13

11th Sunday
1- Ex 19:2-6a
2- Rom 5:6-11
3- Mt 9:36--10:8

12th Sunday
1- Jer 20:10-13
2- Rom 5:12-15
3- Mt 10:26-33

13th Sunday
1- 2Kgs 4:8-11,14-16a
2- Rom 6:3-4,8-11
3- Mt 10:37-42

14th Sunday
1- Zech 9:9-10
2- Rom 8:9,11-13
3- Mt 11:25-30

15th Sunday
1- Isa 55:10-11
2- Rom 8:18-23
3- Mt 13:1-23

16th Sunday
1- Wisdom 12:13,16-19
2- Rom 8:26-27
3- Mt 13:24-43

17th Sunday
1- 1Kgs 3:5,7-12
2- Rom 8:28-30
3- Mt 13:44-52

18th Sunday
1- Isa 55:1-3
2- Rom 8:35,37-39
3- Mt 14:13-21

19th Sunday
1- 1Kgs 19:9a,11-13a
2- Rom 9:1-5
3- Mt 14:22-33

20th Sunday
1- Isa 56:1,6-7
2- Rom 11:13-15,29-32
3- Mt 15:21-28

21st Sunday
1- Isa 22:19-23
2- Rom 11:33-36
3- Mt 16:13-20

22nd Sunday
1- Jer 20:7-9
2- Rom 12:1-2
3- Mt 16:21-27

23rd Sunday
1- Ezek 33:7-9
2- Rom 13:8-10
3- Mt 18:15-20

24th Sunday
1- Sirach 27:30--28:7
2- Rom 14:7-9
3- Mt 18:21-35

25th Sunday
 1- Isa 55:6-9
 2- Phil 1:20c-24,27a
 3- Mt 20:1-16a

26th Sunday
 1- Ezek 18:25-28
 2- Phil 2:1-11
 3- Mt 21:28-32

27th Sunday
 1- Isa 5:1-7
 2- Phil 4:6-9
 3- Mt 21:33-43

28th Sunday
 1- Isa 25:6-10a
 2- Phil 4:12-14,19-20
 3- Mt 22:1-14

29th Sunday
 1- Isa 45:1,4-6
 2- 1Thes 1:1-5b
 3- Mt 22:15-21

30th Sunday
 1- Ex 22:20-26
 2- 1Thes 1:5c-10
 3- Mt 22:34-40

31st Sunday
 1- Mal 1:14b--2:2b,8-10
 2- 1Thes 2:7b-9,13
 3- Mt 23:1-12

32nd Sunday
 1- Wisdom 6:12-16
 2- 1Thes 4:13-18
 3- Mt 25:1-13

33rd Sunday
 1- Prov 31:10-13,19-20,30-31
 2- 1Thes 5:1-6
 3- Mt 25:14-30

34th Sunday (Christ the King)
 1- Ezek 34:11-12,15-17
 2- 1Cor 15:20-26,28
 3- Mt 25:31-46

CYCLE B

Cycle of Sunday Readings
2009, 2012, 2015

Advent Season
1st Sunday of Advent
  1- Isa 63:16b-17,19b; 64:2b-7
  2- 1Cor 1:3-9
  3- Mk 13:33-37

2nd Sunday of Advent
  1- Isa 40:1-5,9-11
  2- 2Pt 3:8-14
  3- Mk 1:1-8

3rd Sunday of Advent
  1- Isa 61:1-2a,10-11
  2- 1Thes 5:16-24
  3- Jn 1:6-8,19-28

4th Sunday of Advent
  1- 2Sam 7:1-5,8b-11,16
  2- Rom 16:25-27
  3- Lk 1:26-38

Christmas Season
Christmas Vigil
  1- Isa 62:1-5
  2- Acts 13:16-17,22-25
  3- Mt 1:1-25

Christmas (At Midnight)
  1- Isa 9:1-6
  2- Ti 2:11-14
  3- Lk 2:1-14

Christmas (At Dawn)
  1- Isa 62:11-12
  2- Ti 3:4-7
  3- Lk 2:15-20

Christmas (During the Day)
  1- Isa 52:7-10
  2- Heb 1:1-6
  3- Jn 1:1-18

Sunday After Christmas
(Holy Family)
  1- Gen 15:1-6; 21:1-3
  2- Heb 11:8,11-12,17-19
  3- Lk 2:22-40

January 1 (Solemnity of Mary,
Mother of God)
  1- Num 6:22-27
  2- Gal 4:4-7
  3- Lk 2:16-21

2nd Sunday After Christmas
  1- Sirach 24:1-2,8-12
  2- Eph 1:3-6,15-18
  3- Jn 1:1-18

Epiphany
1- Isa 60:1-6
2- Eph 3:2-3a,5-6
3- Mt 2:1-12

Sunday After Epiphany
(Baptism of the Lord)
1- Isa 42:1-4,6-7
2- Acts 10:34-38
3- Mk 1:6b-11

Lenten Season
Ash Wednesday
1- Joel 2:12-18
2- 2Cor 5:20--6:2
3- Mt 6:1-6,16-18

1st Sunday of Lent
1- Gen 9:8-15
2- 1Pt 3:18-22
3- Mk 1:12-15

2nd Sunday of Lent
1- Gen 22:1-2,9a,10-13,15-18
2- Rom 8:31b-34
3- Mk 9:2-10

3rd Sunday of Lent
1- Ex 20:1-17
2- 1Cor 1:22-25
3- Jn 2:13-25

4th Sunday of Lent
1- 2Chron 36:14-16,19-23
2- Eph 2:4-10
3- Jn 3:14-21

5th Sunday of Lent
1- Jer 31:31-34
2- Heb 5:7-9
3- Jn 12:20-33

Passion Sunday (Palm Sunday)
Procession: Mk 11:1-10
or Jn 12:12-16
1- Isa 50:4-7
2- Phil 2:6-11
3- Mk 14:1--15:47

Easter Triduum & Easter Season
Mass of Lord's Supper
1- Ex 12:1-8,11-14
2- 1Cor 11:23-26
3- Jn 13:1-15

Good Friday
1- Isa 52:13--53:12
2- Heb 4:14-16; 5:7-9
3- Jn 18:1--19:42

Easter Vigil
1- Gen 1:1--2:2
Gen 22:1-18
Ex 14:15--15:1
Isa 54:5-14
Isa 55:1-11
Baruch 3:9-15,32--4:4
Ezek 36:16-28
2- Rom 6:3-11
3- Mk 16:1-8

Easter Sunday
1- Acts 10:34a,37-43
2- Col 3:1-4
or 1 Col 5:6b-8
3- Jn 20:1-9
or Mk 16:1-8
Evening: 3- Lk 24:13-35

2nd Sunday of Easter
1- Acts 4:32-35
2- 1Jn 5:1-6
3- Jn 20:19-31

3rd Sunday of Easter
  1- Acts 3:13-15,17-19
  2- 1Jn 2:1-5a
  3- Lk 24:35-48

4th Sunday of Easter
  1- Acts 4:8-12
  2- 1Jn 3:1-2
  3- Jn 10:11-18

5th Sunday of Easter
  1- Acts 9:26-31
  2- 1Jn 3:18-24
  3- Jn 15:1-8

6th Sunday of Easter
  1- Acts 10:25-26,34-35,44-48
  2- 1Jn 4:7-10
  3- Jn 15:9-17

Ascension of Our Lord
  1- Acts 1:1-11
  2- Eph 1:17-23 or 4:1-13
  3- Mk 16:15-20

7th Sunday of Easter
  1- Acts 1:15-17,20a,20c-26
  2- 1Jn 4:11-16
  3- Jn 17:11b-19

Pentecost Vigil
  1- Gen 11:1-9
  or Ex 19:3-8a,16-20b
  or Ezek 37:1-14
  or Joel 3:1-5
  2- Rom 8:22-27
  3- Jn 7:37-39

Mass of the Day
  1- Acts 2:1-11
  2- 1Cor 12:3b-7,12-13
  3- Jn 20:19-23

Pentecost - Optional
  2- Gal 5:16-25
  3- Jn 15:26-27; 16:12-15

Solemnities of the Lord during Ordinary Time
Trinity Sunday (Sunday after Pentecost)
  1- Deut 4:32-34,39-40
  2- Rom 8:14-17
  3- Mt 28:16-20

Corpus Christi
  1- Ex 24:3-8
  2- Heb 9:11-15
  3- Mk 14:12-16,22-26

Sacred Heart of Jesus
  1- Hosea 11:1,3-4,8c-9
  2- Eph 3:8-12,14-19
  3- Jn 19:31-37

Ordinary Time
1st Sunday (See Baptism of the Lord, above)
2nd Sunday
  1- 1Sam 3:3b-10,19
  2- 1Cor 6:13c-15a,17-20
  3- Jn 1:35-42

3rd Sunday
  1- Jonah 3:1-5,10
  2- 1Cor 7:29-31
  3- Mk 1:14-20

4th Sunday
  1- Deut 18:15-20
  2- 1Cor 7:32-35
  3- Mk 1:21-28

5th Sunday
  1- Job 7:1-4,6-7
  2- 1Cor 9:16-19,22-23
  3- Mk 1:29-39

6th Sunday
1- Lev 13:1-2,45-46
2- 1Cor 10:31--11:1
3- Mk 1:40-45

7th Sunday
1- Isa 43:18-19,21-22,24b-25
2- 2Cor 1:18-22
3- Mk 2:1-12

8th Sunday
1- Hosea 2:16b,17b,21-22
2- 2Cor 3:1b-6
3- Mk 2:18-22

9th Sunday
1- Deut 5:12-15
2- 2Cor 4:6-11
3- Mk 2:23--3:6

10th Sunday
1- Gen 3:9-15
2- 2Cor 4:13--5:1
3- Mk 3:20-35

11th Sunday
1- Ezek 17:22-24
2- 2Cor 5:6-10
3- Mk 4:26-34

12th Sunday
1- Job 38:1,8-11
2- 2Cor 5:14-17
3- Mk 4:35-41

13th Sunday
1- Wisdom 1:13-15; 2:23-24
2- 2Cor 8:7,9,13-15
3- Mk 5:21-43

14th Sunday
1- Ezek 2:2-5
2- 2Cor 12:7-10
3- Mk 6:1-6

15th Sunday
1- Amos 7:12-15
2- Eph 1:3-14
3- Mk 6:7-13

16th Sunday
1- Jer 23:1-6
2- Eph 2:13-18
3- Mk 6:30-34

17th Sunday
1- 2Kgs 4:42-44
2- Eph 4:1-6
3- Jn 6:1-15

18th Sunday
1- Ex 16:2-4,12-15
2- Eph 4:17,20-24
3- Jn 6:24-35

19th Sunday
1- 1Kgs 19:4-8
2- Eph 4:30--5:2
3- Jn 6:41-51

20th Sunday
1- Prov 9:1-6
2- Eph 5:15-20
3- Jn 6:51-58

21st Sunday
1- Josh 24:1-2a,15-17,18b
2- Eph 5:21-32
3- Jn 6:60-69

22nd Sunday
1- Deut 4:1-2,6-8
2- Jms 1:17-18,21b-22,27
3- Mk 7:1-8,14-15,21-23

23rd Sunday
1- Isa 35:4-7a
2- Jms 2:1-5
3- Mk 7:31-37

24th Sunday
1- Isa 50:5-9a
2- Jms 2:14-18
3- Mk 8:27-35

25th Sunday
1- Wisdom 2:12,17-20
2- Jms 3:16--4:3
3- Mk 9:30-37

26th Sunday
1- Num 11:25-29
2- Jms 5:1-6
3- Mk 9:38-43,45,47-48

27th Sunday
1- Gen 2:18-24
2- Heb 2:9-11
3- Mk 10:2-16

28th Sunday
1- Wisdom 7:7-11
2- Heb 4:12-13
3- Mk 10:17-30

29th Sunday
1- Isa 53:10-11
2- Heb 4:14-16
3- Mk 10:35-45

30th Sunday
1- Jer 31:7-9
2- Heb 5:1-6
3- Mk 10:46-53

31st Sunday
1- Deut 6:2-6
2- Heb 7:23-28
3- Mk 12:28b-34

32nd Sunday
1- 1Kgs 17:10-16
2- Heb 9:24-28
3- Mk 12:38-44

33rd Sunday
1- Dan 12:1-3
2- Heb 10:11-14,18
3- Mk 13:24-32

34th Sunday (Christ the King)
1- Dan 7:13-14
2- Rv 1:5-8
3- Jn 18:33b-37

CYCLE C

Cycle of Sunday readings
2010, 2013, 2016

Advent Season
1st Sunday of Advent
  1- Jer 33:14-16
  2- 1Thes 3:12--4:2
  3- Lk 21:25-28,34-36

2nd Sunday of Advent
  1- Baruch 5:1-9
  2- Phil 1:4-6,8-11
  3- Lk 3:1-6

3rd Sunday of Advent
  1- Zeph 3:14-18a
  2- Phil 4:4-7
  3- Lk 3:10-18

4th Sunday of Advent
  1- Micah 5:1-4a
  2- Heb 10:5-10
  3- Lk 1:39-45

Christmas Season
Christmas Vigil
  1- Isa 62:1-6
  2- Acts 13:16-17,22-25
  3- Mt 1:1-25

Christmas (At Midnight)
  1- Isa 9:1-6
  2- Ti 2:11-14
  3- Lk 2:1-14

Christmas (At Dawn)
  1- Isa 62:11-12
  2- Ti 3:4-7
  3- Lk 2:15-20

Christmas (During the Day)
  1- Isa 57:7-10
  2- Heb 1:1-6
  3- Jn 1:1-18

Sunday After Christmas
(Holy Family)
  1- 1 Sam 1:19b-22,24-28
  2- 1Jn 3:1-2,21-24
  3- Lk 2:41-52

January 1 (Solemnity of Mary,
Mother of God)
  1- Num 6:22-27
  2- Gal 4:4-7
  3- Lk 2:16-21

2nd Sunday After Christmas
  1- Sirach 24:1-2,8-12
  2- Eph 1:3-6,15-18
  3- Jn 1:1-18

Epiphany
1- Isa 60:1-6
2- Eph 3:2-3a,5-6
3- Mt 2:1-12

Sunday After Epiphany
(Baptism of the Lord)
1- Isa 42:1-4,6-7
2- Acts 10:34-38
3- Lk 3:15-16,21-22

Lenten Season
Ash Wednesday
1- Joel 2:12-18
2- 2Cor 5:20--6:2
3- Mt 6:1-6,16-18

1st Sunday of Lent
1- Deut 26:4-10
2- Rom 10:8-13
3- Lk 4:1-13

2nd Sunday of Lent
1- Gen 15:5-12,17-18
2- Phil 3:17--4:1
3- Lk 9:28b-36

3rd Sunday of Lent
1- Ex 3:1-8a,13-15
2- 1Cor 10:1-6,10-12
3- Lk 13:1-9

4th Sunday of Lent
1- Josh 5:9a,10-12
2- 2Cor 5:17-21
3- Lk 15:1-3,11-32

5th Sunday of Lent
1- Isa 43:16-21
2- Phil 3:8-14
3- Jn 8:1-11

Passion Sunday (Palm Sunday)
Procession: Lk 19:28-40
1- Isa 50:4-7
2- Phil 2:6-11
3- Lk 22:14--23:56

Easter Triduum & Easter Season
Mass of Lord's Supper
1- Ex 12:1-8,11-14
2- 1Cor 11:23-26
3- Jn 13:1-15

Good Friday
1- Isa 52:13--53:12
2- Heb 4:14-16; 5:7-9
3- Jn 18:1--19:42

Easter Vigil
1- Gen 1:1--2:2
Gen 22:1-18
Ex 14:15--15:1
Isa 54:5-14
Isa 55:1-11
Baruch 3:9-15,32--4:4
Ezek 36:16-28
2- Rom 6:3-11
3- Lk 24:1-12

Easter Sunday
1- Acts 10:34a,37-43
2- Col 3:1-4
or 1Cor 5:6b-8
3- Jn 20:1-9
or Lk 24:1-12
Evening: 3 Lk 24:13-35

2nd Sunday of Easter
1- Acts 5:12-16
2- Rv 1:9-11a,12-13,17-19
3- Jn 20:19-31

3rd Sunday of Easter
1- Acts 5:27b-32,40b-41
2- Rv 5:11-14
3- Jn 21:1-19

4th Sunday of Easter
  1- Acts 13:14,43-52
  2- Rv 7:9,14b-17
  3- Jn 10:27-30

5th Sunday of Easter
  1- Acts 14:21-27
  2- Rv 21:1-5a
  3- Jn 13:31-33a,34-35

6th Sunday of Easter
  1- Acts 15:1-2,22-29
  2- Rv 21:10-14,22-23
  3- Jn 14:23-29

Ascension of the Lord
  1- Acts 1:1-11
  2- Eph 1:17-23
  or Heb 9:24-28; 10:19-23
  3- Lk 24:46-53

7th Sunday of Easter
  1- Acts 7:55-60
  2- Rv 22:12-14,16-17,20
  3- Jn 17:20-26

Pentecost Vigil
  1- Gen 11:1-9
  or Ex 19:3-8a,16-20b
  or Ezek 37:1-14
  or Joel 3:1-5
  2- Rom 8:22-27
  3- Jn 7:37-39

Mass of the Day
  1- Acts 2:1-11
  2- 1Cor 12:3b-7,12-13
  or Rom 8:8-27
  3- Jn 20:19-23
  or Jn 14:15-16,23b-26

Solemnities of the Lord During Ordinary

Trinity Sunday (Sunday After Pentecost)
  1- Prov 8:22-31
  2- Rom 5:1-5
  3- Jn 16:12-15

Corpus Christi
  1- Gen 14:18-20
  2- 1Cor 11:23-26
  3- Lk 9:11b-17

Sacred Heart of Jesus
  1- Ezek 34:11-16
  2- Rom 5:5-11
  3- Lk 15:3-7

Ordinary Time

1st Sunday (See Baptism of the Lord, above)

2nd Sunday
  1- Isa 62:1-5
  2- 1Cor 12:4-11
  3- Jn 2:1-12

3rd Sunday
  1- Neh 8:1-4a,5-6,8-10
  2- 1Cor 12:12-30
  3- Lk 1:1-4; 4:14-21

4th Sunday
  1- Jer 1:4-5,17-19
  2- 1Cor 12:31--13:13
  3- Lk 4:21-30

5th Sunday
  1- Isa 6:1-2a,3-8
  2- 1Cor 15:1-11
  3- Lk 5:1-11

6th Sunday
  1- Jer 17:5-8
  2- 1Cor 15:12,16-20
  3- Lk 6:17,20-26

7th Sunday
  1- 1Sam 26:2,7-9,12-13,22-23
  2- 1Cor 15:45-49
  3- Lk 6:27-38

8th Sunday
  1- Sirach 27:4-7
  2- 1Cor 15:54-58
  3- Lk 6:39-45

9th Sunday
  1- 1Kgs 8:41-43
  2- Gal 1:1-2,6-10
  3- Lk 7:1-10

10th Sunday
  1- 1Kgs 17:17-24
  2- Gal 1:11-19
  3- Lk 7:11-17

11th Sunday
  1- 2Sam 12:7-10,13
  2- Gal 2:16,19-21
  3- Lk 7:36--8:3

12th Sunday
  1- Zech 12:10-11
  2- Gal 3:26-29
  3- Lk 9:18-24

13th Sunday
  1- 1Kgs 19:16b,19-21
  2- Gal 5:1,13-18
  3- Lk 9:51-62

14th Sunday
  1- Isa 66:10-14c
  2- Gal 6:14-18
  3- Lk 10:1-12,17-20

15th Sunday
  1- Deut 30:10-14
  2- Col 1:15-20
  3- Lk 10:25-37

16th Sunday
  1- Gen 18:1-10a
  2- Col 1:24-28
  3- Lk 10:38-42

17th Sunday
  1- Gen 18:20-32
  2- Col 2:12-14
  3- Lk 11:1-13

18th Sunday
  1- Eccl 1:2; 2:21-23
  2- Col 3:1-5,9-11
  3- Lk 12:13-31

19th Sunday
  1- Wisdom 18:6-9
  2- Heb 11:1-2,8-19
  3- Lk 12:32-48

20th Sunday
  1- Jer 38:4-6,8-10
  2- Heb 12:1-4
  3- Lk 12:49-53

21st Sunday
  1- Isa 66:18-21
  2- Heb 12:5-7,11-13
  3- Lk 13:22-30

22nd Sunday
  1- Sirach 3:17-18,20,28-29
  2- Heb 12:18-19,22-24a
  3- Lk 14:1,7-14

23rd Sunday
  1- Wisdom 9:13-18b
  2- Phlm 1:9b-10,12-17
  3- Lk 14:25-33

24th Sunday
  1- Ex 32:7-11,13-14
  2- 1Tm 1:12-17
  3- Lk 15:1-32

25th Sunday
1- Amos 8:4-7
2- 1Tm 2:1-8
3- Lk 16:1-13

26th Sunday
1- Amos 6:la,4-7
2- 1Tm 6:11-16
3- Lk 16:19-31

27th Sunday
1- Hab 1:2-3; 2:2-4
2- 2Tm 1:6-8,13-14
3- Lk 17:5-10

28th Sunday
1- 2Kgs 5:14-17
2- 2Tm 2:8-13
3- Lk 17:11-19

29th Sunday
1- Ex 17:8-13
2- 2Tm 3:14--4:2
3- Lk 18:1-8

30th Sunday
1- Sirach 35:12-14,16-18
2- 2Tm 4:6-8,16-18
3- Lk 18:9-14

31st Sunday
1- Wisdom 11:23--12:2
2- 2Thes 1:11--2:2
3- Lk 19:1-10

32nd Sunday
1- 2Macc 7:1-2,9-14
2- 2Thes 2:16--3:5
3- Lk 20:27-38

33rd Sunday
1- Mal 3:19-20a
2- 2Thes 3:7-12
3- Lk 21:5-19

34th Sunday (Christ the King)
1- 2Sam 5:1-3
2- Col 1:12-20
3- Lk 23:35-43

Ever get "lost" during the Sunday readings? Well, Life Teen is here to help with their "Sunday, Sunday, Sunday" podcast!

Every week, Life Teen International's Mark Hart (a.k.a. the "Bible Geek"®) puts Sunday scripture into simple words, clarifying their meaning with practical insights and just a touch of humor.

To hear the free weekly "Sunday, Sunday, Sunday" podcast, visit www.lifeteen.com (to listen online) or subscribe through iTunes by searching "lifeteen.com"— your weekly podcast will be delivered straight to your iTunes account.

Understanding scripture has never been easier! Subscribe today!

www.lifeteen.com

THEMATIC CONCORDANCE OF PAUL'S WRITINGS

Want to see for yourself what the Holy Spirit moved through St. Paul had to share about the following topics?

Take the time to read and pray through them on your own.

ANGER
- Ephesians 4:26
- Ephesians 4:31
- Colossians 3:8
- Colossians 3:19
- 1 Timothy 2:8

CHASTITY/SEXUALITY
- Romans 6:12-13
- Romans 12:1
- Romans 13:13
- 1 Corinthians 6:9
- 1 Corinthians 6:15
- 2 Corinthians 12:21
- Galatians 5:19
- Ephesians 4:19
- 1 Thessalonians 4:5

CHURCH/COMMUNITY
- Romans 12:4-5
- 1 Corinthians 10:17
- 1 Corinthians 12:12-13
- 1 Corinthians 12:20
- Ephesians 4:3-4
- Colossians 3:15
- Philippians 1:27

DATING
- 2 Corinthians 6:14
- 2 Corinthians 7:1
- Galatians 5:23
- 1 Thessalonians 4:3-4
- 1 Thessalonians 4:7
- 1 Timothy 2:9
- 2 Timothy 1:7

DEATH
- Romans 5:10,12,14,17 and 21
- Romans 6:3-4, 9-10, 23
- Romans 8:2, 6
- 1 Corinthians 15:21,54-55
- 2 Corinthians 1:9-10
- 2 Corinthians 4:12
- 2 Corinthians 7:10
- Philippians 1:21
- Philippians 2:8
- Philippians 3:10
- Colossians 3:5

DISCIPLESHIP
- Romans 4:16
- 2 Corinthians 7:1
- Galatians 2:20
- Galatians 5:25
- Galatians 6:16
- Ephesians 4:24
- 1 Thessalonians 3:13
- 1 Thessalonians 4:3-4,7
- 2 Timothy 1:9

DOUBT
- Romans 4:20
- Romans 6:8
- Galatians 3:22
- Ephesians 1:19
- Philippians 1:29
- 1 Thessalonians 4:14
- 1 Timothy 1:16

DRINKING/PARTYING
- Romans 2:19
- Romans 13:12-13
- 1 Corinthians 4:5
- 1 Corinthians 15:34
- 1 Thessalonians 5:8
- Galatians 5:21
- Ephesians 5:8,11
- Ephesians 6:12

ETERNAL LIFE
- Romans 2:7
- Romans 5:21
- Romans 6:23
- Galatians 6:8
- Philippians 3:20
- Colossians 1:5, 16, 20
- 1 Timothy 1:2
- 1 Timothy 6:12

EUCHARIST
- 1 Corinthians 10:16-17
- 1 Corinthians 11:23, 26-28
- Ephesians 2:13
- Ephesians 5:30
- Colossians 1:20

EVANGELIZATION
- 1 Corinthians 9:12, 23
- 2 Corinthians 1:7
- Philippians 2:17-18
- 1 Thessalonians 2:8
- 1 Timothy 6:18
- 2 Timothy 1:8
- 2 Timothy 2:3

FAITH
- Romans 1:12, 17
- Romans 3:28, 31
- Romans 4:16, 20
- Romans 5:2
- Romans 10:17
- Romans 12:6
- 1 Corinthians 2:5
- 1 Corinthians 13:13
- 1 Corinthians 15:14, 17
- 2 Corinthians 5:7
- Galatians 2:20
- Galatians 3:23
- Galatians 5:5
- Ephesians 2:8
- Ephesians 3:12, 17
- Ephesians 6:16
- Colossians 1:4
- 1 Thessalonians 3:7, 10
- 2 Thessalonians 1:3-4
- 1 Timothy 1:5
- 1 Timothy 4:12
- 1 Timothy 6:12
- 2 Timothy 4:7

FAMILY
- Romans 8:14, 16-17, 19, 21
- Galatians 3:26
- Galatians 4:6
- Galatians 6:10
- Ephesians 3:15
- Ephesians 5:1
- Ephesians 6:1, 4
- Philippians 2:15
- 1 Thessalonians 2:11
- 1 Thessalonians 5:5
- 1 Timothy 3:4
- 1 Timothy 5:4, 8

FEAR
- Romans 8:15
- 2 Corinthians 5:6-8
- Ephesians 6:20
- Philippians 1:20
- 1 Thessalonians 2:2
- 2 Timothy 1:7

FUTURE/VOCATION
- Romans 8:28, 38
- Romans 9:21
- Ephesians 1:11
- Ephesians 2:10
- Philippians 2:13
- 2 Thessalonians 1:11
- 1 Timothy 6:19

GOD THE FATHER
- Romans 8:15
- 1 Corinthians 8:6
- Galatians 4:6
- Ephesians 2:18
- Ephesians 3:14
- Ephesians 5:20
- Philippians 2:11
- Colossians 3:17

GRACE
- Romans 1:5
- Romans 3:24
- Romans 5:2, 20-21
- Romans 6:1, 14-15
- Romans 11:6
- 1 Corinthians 15:10
- 2 Corinthians 6:1
- 2 Corinthians 9:8, 14
- 2 Corinthians 12:9
- Galatians 2:21
- Ephesians 4:7, 29
- Philippians 4:23
- 2 Timothy 2:1

GREED/MATERIALISM

- Romans 1:29
- Romans 7:7
- Ephesians 5:3
- Colossians 3:5
- 1 Timothy 3:3
- 1 Timothy 6:10

HOLY SPIRIT

- Romans 5:5
- Romans 5:2, 4-5
- Romans 8:24-25
- Romans 14:17
- Romans 15:16
- 1 Corinthians 6:19
- 1 Corinthians 12:3
- 1 Corinthians 13:13
- 2 Corinthians 1:7, 10
- 2 Corinthians 3:12
- 2 Corinthians 13:13
- Ephesians 1:13
- Ephesians 4:4
- Philippians 3:12
- Colossians 1:5, 23, 27
- 1 Thessalonians 1:5-6
- 1 Thessalonians 4:8
- 1 Timothy 4:10
- 2 Timothy 1:14
- Titus 1:2

JUDGMENT

- Romans 2:1-2
- Romans 5:12
- Romans 14:3-4, 10
- 1 Corinthians 2:15
- 1 Corinthians 4:3, 5
- 1 Corinthians 6:2
- 2 Thessalonians 1:5
- 1 Timothy 5:24
- 2 Timothy 4:1
- 2 Timothy 4:8

LOVE

- Romans 5:5, 8
- Romans 8:35, 39
- Romans 12:9-10
- Romans 13:8, 10
- 1 Corinthians 2:9
- 1 Corinthians 13:1-13
- 2 Corinthians 5:14
- 2 Corinthians 13:13
- Galatians 5:6
- Galatians 5:22
- Ephesians 2:4
- Ephesians 5:2
- Philippians 1:9
- Colossians 3:14
- 1 Thessalonians 5:8
- 1 Timothy 4:12
- 2 Timothy 1:7

MARRIAGE

- 1 Corinthians 7:3-4, 10-13
- 1 Corinthians 7:14, 16
- 1 Corinthians 11:2-3
- Ephesians 5:23-25, 28, 33
- Colossians 3:18-19
- 1 Thessalonians 4:4

PRAYER

- Romans 8:26
- Romans 12:12
- 1 Corinthians 7:5
- 1 Corinthians 14:14-15
- Ephesians 6:18
- Philippians 1:9
- Philippians 4:6
- Colossians 4:2
- 1 Thessalonians 5:17
- 1 Timothy 2:8
- 1 Timothy 4:5

PRIESTHOOD/ AUTHORITY

- Romans 1:5
- 1 Corinthians 7:35
- 1 Corinthians 9:23
- 1 Corinthians 15:5
- 2 Corinthians 4:11
- 2 Corinthians 12:10
- Galatians 1:18
- Philippians 1:29
- Philippians 2:30
- 1 Timothy 3:1-2
- 1 Timothy 5:17
- Titus 1:7

SALVATION

- Romans 1:16
- Romans 5:9-10
- Romans 8:24
- Romans 13:11
- 1 Corinthians 3:15
- 2 Corinthians 6:2
- Ephesians 1:13
- Philippians 2:12
- 1 Thessalonians 5:8-9
- 1Timothy 2:4
- 2 Timothy 3:15

SIN

- Romans 5:12-14
- Romans 6:11-12, 14, 22-23
- Romans 7:17, 20
- Romans 8:10
- 1 Corinthians 6:18
- 1 Corinthians 8:13
- 1 Corinthians 15:56
- 2 Corinthians 5:21

TEMPTATION

- Romans 7:19, 21
- 1 Corinthians 7:5
- 1 Corinthians 10:6, 13
- 1 Corinthians 14:20
- Galatians 6:1
- Ephesians 6:12-13
- Colossians 3:5
- 1 Thessalonians 3:3
- 1 Thessalonians 5:22
- 2 Thessalonians 3:3
- 1 Timothy 6:9
- 2 Timothy 4:18

THE WISDOM OF GOD
THROUGH THE PEN OF PAUL

VERSES FOR REFLECTION FROM ST. PAUL

Saul was a man who knew the power of words. Spend time praying and journaling these fifty verses from St. Paul over the next couple of months. You will soon see that the Holy Spirit not only spoke through him (as demonstrated here), but that the Holy Spirit will begin speaking through you, too, in all new ways.

Romans 1:16
Romans 2:5-8
Romans 6:4
Romans 8:16-18
Romans 8:28
Romans 8:35-39
Romans 12:1
Romans 15:30
Romans 16:7
1 Corinthians 1:10
1 Corinthians 3:15
1 Corinthians 6:16
1 Corinthians 10:13
1 Corinthians 11:1-2
1 Corinthians 11:23-29
1 Corinthians 12:11
1 Corinthians 13:2

2 Corinthians 2:5
2 Corinthians 5:17-20
2 Corinthians 11:15
Galatians 2:20
Galatians 4:4
Galatians 5:4
Galatians 5:6
Ephesians 1:13
Ephesians 1:7
Ephesians 2:1-3
Ephesians 2:10
Ephesians 5:22-32
Ephesians 6:18-10
Philippians 2:2
Philippians 2:12
Philippians 3:13-14
Philippians 4:13

Colossians 1:24
Colossians 2:9
Colossians 3:17
Colossians 3:24-25
1 Thessalonians 5:2-3
1 Thessalonians 5:8
1 Thessalonians 5:17
2 Thessalonians 2:15
1 Timothy 3:15
1 Timothy 4:12
1 Timothy 4:13
2 Timothy 1:9
2 Timothy 1:13
2 Timothy 2:11-13
2 Timothy 3:16
2 Timothy 4:3

RESOURCES FOR FURTHER STUDY

Cameron, Fr. Peter John (ed). *Praying with Saint Paul: Daily Reflections on the Letters of the Apostle Paul* (San Francisco: Ignatius, 2008).

Hahn, Scott. *A Father Who Keeps His Promises: God's Covenant Love in Scripture* (Ann Arbor, MI: Servant, 1998).

Answering Common Objections (CD set [St. Joseph Communications]).

Romanism in Romans: A Bible Study of the Book of Romans (CD set [St. Joseph Communications]).

Salvation History (CD set [St. Joseph Communications]).

The Mystery: A Bible Study of the Book of Ephesians (CD set [St. Joseph Communications]).

Understanding The Scriptures: A Complete Course On Bible Study (Chicago: Midwest Theological Forum, 2005).

Ignatius Catholic Study Bible: The Acts of the Apostles, with Curtis Mitch (San Francisco: Ignatius Press, 2002).

Ignatius Catholic Study Bible: The First and Second Letters of Saint Paul to the Corinthians, with Curtis Mitch (San Francisco: Ignatius Press, 2004).

Ignatius Catholic Study Bible: The Letters of St. Paul to the Galatians and Ephesians, with Curtis Mitch (San Francisco: Ignatius Press, 2005).

Ignatius Catholic Study Bible: The Letters of St. Paul to the Philippians, Colossians, and Philemon, with Curtis Mitch (San Francisco: Ignatius Press, 2005).

Ignatius Catholic Study Bible: The Letter of Saint Paul to the Romans, with Curtis Mitch (San Francisco: Ignatius Press, 2003).

Ignatius Catholic Study Bible: The Letters of St. Paul to the Thessalonians, Timothy, and Titus, with Curtis Mitch (San Francisco: Ignatius Press, 2005).

Pacwa, Mitch. *St. Paul: Jubilee Year of the Apostle Paul Edition: A Bible Study for Catholics* (Huntington, IN: Our Sunday Visitor, 2008).

Pitre, Brant. *The Apostle Paul: Unlocking the Mysteries of His Theology* (CD set [Catholic Productions]).

*Wright, N.T. *Paul: In Fresh Perspective* (Minneapolis: Fortress Press, 2005).

What Saint Paul Really Said: Was Paul of Tarsus the Real Founder of Christianity? (Grand Rapids: Eerdmans, 1997).

Wright, Tom. *Acts for Everyone: Part One* (Louisville, KY: Westminster John Knox Press, 2007).

Acts for Everyone: Part Two (Louisville, KY: Westminster John Knox Press, 2008).

Paul for Everyone: 1 Corinthians (Louisville, KY: Westminster John Knox Press, 2004).

Paul for Everyone: 2 Corinthians (Louisville, KY: Westminster John Knox Press, 2004).

Paul for Everyone: Galatians and Thessalonians (Louisville, KY: Westminster John Knox Press, 2004).

Paul for Everyone: The Pastoral Letters (Louisville, KY: Westminster John Knox Press, 2004).

Paul for Everyone: The Prison Letters (Louisville, KY: Westminster John Knox Press, 2004).

Paul for Everyone: Romans: Part One (Louisville, KY: Westminster John Knox Press, 2004).

Paul for Everyone: Romans: Part Two (Louisville, KY: Westminster John Knox Press, 2004).

* [Note: N.T. ("Tom") Wright is one of the most brilliant "Pauline" scholars in the world today. His research has done much to help further the understanding of St. Paul. We recommend his books even though he is not a Catholic (N.T. Wright is an Anglican Bishop), with the understanding that the official teaching of the Catholic Church is to be followed at all times on all topics. All of the other authors are Catholic.]

LIFE TEEN MISSION STATEMENT

Life Teen, Inc. is an international Catholic Ministry that serves the Church and leads all teens closer to Christ by providing resources and training that encourage vibrant Eucharistic celebrations and opportunities for teens to grow in their faith.

2222 S. Dobson Rd. Suite 601, Mesa, AZ 85202
1-800-809-3902   www.lifeteen.com

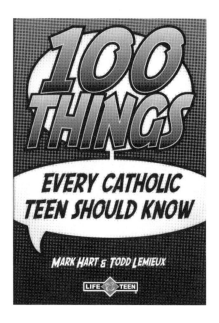

Do you wonder why, as Catholics, we do some of the things that we do? Do you ever find yourself wishing for short, simple answers as to what the Church teaches and why we claim it as truth?

Let *100 Things Every Catholic Teen Should Know* bring to light a bunch of things you might already know and a ton of stuff you probably don't. You won't get long, boring answers; you will get quick, straight answers with 100% truth.

Mary Hart and Todd Lemieux have an undeniably unique way to make the most controversial and complicated Church teachings, entertaining and effortless to follow. Let these two authors show you not only how great it is to be Catholic, but how fun it is to be Catholic, as well.

So, prepare for an overview of Catholicism that is sure to leave you a little smarter and a lot more confident.

To order copies visit www.lifeteen.com

Saintbook

Oftentimes, the Blessed Virgin Mary and the Communion of Saints are a source of confusion and debate for Catholics and non-Catholics. *Saintbook* is a powerful tool to eliminate confusion and misconceptions and bring the Catholic truth to light. *Saintbook* explains why Catholics have such a special devotion to Mary, her specific role in the Church and answers the most hotly contested questions regarding her prayers. In addition, *Saintbook* walks the reader through the Rosary, offering instruction and reflection on all twenty mysteries.

You'll also take a closer look at over fifty saints, with biographies, stories and explanations of the lives they led and the process of becoming a saint. You can follow along throughout the year with special feast days, investigate special patrons and read more about how you, like Mary and the Saints are "set apart" and called to be a living witness in the world today. This is a fantastic resource and gift for any Catholic, young or young-at-heart and for anyone preparing for Confirmation, enrolled in RCIA or even cradle Catholics just looking to deepen their prayer life and knowledge of the Catholic faith.

To order copies visit www.lifeteen.com